In Service to America

AICS at 75

In Service to America
AICS at 75

George J. Petrello, Ph.D.
Dean and Professor of Management
Andreas School of Business
Barry University

WITH SPECIAL ASSISTANCE BY

Mary B. Wine
Association of Independent Colleges and Schools

Gregg Division   McGRAW-HILL BOOK COMPANY

New York   Atlanta   Dallas   St. Louis   San Francisco
Auckland   Bogotá   Guatemala   Hamburg   Lisbon
London   Madrid   Mexico   Milan   Montreal   New Delhi
Panama   Paris   San Juan   São Paulo   Singapore
Sydney   Tokyo   Toronto

Co-developed by McGraw-Hill
Book Company and Visual
Education Corporation

McGraw-Hill Book Company
Editor: Richard P. Reskow
Editing Director: Katharine Glynn
Production Director: Frank Bellantoni
Art Director: Karen Tureck
Marketing Manager: Robert Gosdeck

Visual Education Corporation
Project Editor: Jewel Moulthrop
Production Supervisor: Dale Anderson
Photo Research: Ellen Horan,
 Imagefinders
Cover Photo: John Fogle/The Picture
 Cube
Cover Design: Max Crandall

Library of Congress Cataloging-in-Publication Data

Petrello, George J.
 In service to America.

 1. Association of Independent Colleges and
Schools—History. I. Title.
LB2301.P46 1987   378'.04   87-22617
ISBN 0-07-049604-8

1 2 3 4 5 6 7 8 9 0 KGPKGP
8 9 4 3 2 1 0 9 8 7

ISBN 0-07-049604-8

ACKNOWLEDGMENTS

The research and writing of this volume have been a labor of love for me. My affiliation with AICS goes back to 1975, and the opportunity to explore the historical development and future direction of the Association has added a whole new dimension to that affiliation.

I first want to thank Dr. Jerry Miller, President of the Association of Independent Colleges and Schools and the management of McGraw-Hill Book Company, for their invitation to undertake this project. Their confidence in me has been enormously encouraging and helpful in completing the task on time.

The Advisory Committee to the 75th Anniversary book, appointed by Jerry Miller, has been an invaluable help. Through their phone calls, letters and personal contacts, I have gained a wealth of insights that can only be gotten from those who have had firsthand experience. To them I owe my deepest gratitude.

To Mary B. Wine, a long-time AICS professional staff person and member of the 75th Anniversary Advisory Committee, I express special appreciation. Mary served as AICS coordinator and special consultant. We could not have completed the book in so short a time without the devotion, time, and effort that Mary put into the project. Her help will never be forgotten.

Finally, I am grateful to Steve Weissenborn, an MBA student at the Andreas School of Business, Barry University, for his editorial and word processing assistance.

Happy 75th Birthday to the Association of Independent Colleges and Schools! I am pleased and honored to be able to make this contribution to the celebration of your Diamond Jubilee.

—George J. Petrello, Ph.D.

Contents

From the Publisher

The history of the Association of Independent Colleges and Schools is unparalleled in the annals of education. It is the inspiring story of individual schools that were attempting to deal with rapidly changing needs—and that united to achieve some extraordinary results.

AICS has successfully fused the two worlds of education and industry, training its students for professions that were undergoing change as rapidly as the technology of the times. For seventy-five years, AICS and its member schools have focused their attention on the employment needs of the community. Thousands of successful graduates bear testimony to the enormous contribution AICS schools have made, not only in the United States but throughout the world.

We at McGraw-Hill salute you as you celebrate your organization's seventy-fifth anniversary. Our involvement with AICS dates back many years. We have worked with you in conducting Faculty Development Workshops, and we have given our support to countless other AICS endeavors. We are delighted to have been entrusted with the publication of this commemorative book.

The future of AICS is bright indeed, and we look forward to working with you to meet the many challenges that lie ahead.

McGraw-Hill Book Company

From the Chairman

We are celebrating the seventy-fifth anniversary of a great organization, one dedicated to educational excellence, one with a great vision of the future.

These are exciting times in which we celebrate our Diamond Jubilee! Our success is in direct proportion to what we do best—educating our students for specific careers in the marketplace. We know exactly what we are doing and we stand always accountable for our successes. We recruit highly motivated young people; we develop their minds and skills in modern facilities with state-of-the-art equipment; we encourage and enliven them, and help them develop confidence. Then we help them find their own ground, their place of importance, *their career*. Few organizations can do so much for so many in such an efficient way. We have always done this, and do so now, as this book testifies.

We will continue our proud tradition of serving our local communities, perpetuate our collective independence, and respond to change in the global and local economies. We will not imitate other postsecondary schools; rather, we will maintain our unique role as the leaders in private career education in the future as we have done in the past.

Our association began 75 years ago, a seedling in the soil of American education. And now, with 1100 schools and over 750,000 students, we have become a great, endlessly-blossoming tree of career education.

Indeed, we are destined. We will become stronger as we strive for a more developed faculty truly committed to the professional growth of students. We will become known throughout our nation and the world for our performance, our facilities, and our concern for each student. We are destined, as our history shows.

What exciting times! Go forward, continue the work our forefathers began. Accept with me the greatest challenge of all—educating our youth for a prosperous, free society.

—JOHN T. SOUTH, JR.

From the President

Dr. George Petrello and his associates have, with great insight understanding, and flair, chronicled the history of an association whose activities over three-quarters of a century have advanced the national interest, the interests of its member institutions, and the interests of the students they serve. It is a story that makes one proud to be part of the private career school sector of postsecondary education. It is a story that makes us grateful for the extraordinary leadership, vision, and dedication of the volunteers and staff who have shaped the organization.

This elegant book is principally a story about the Association, but it reflects, at the same time, the phenomenal history of resilient and tenacious institutions that have grown dramatically and provided educational services vital to the nation and its economy.

Theoretically at least, taxpaying private career schools face insurmountable odds competing in an environment previously dominated by tax-exempt and taxpayer-subsidized institutions. Why, then, have they grown to the point where today they educate three of every four vocational students at the postsecondary level?

There are many reasons for the success of private career schools, but the most important of these is their responsiveness to the marketplace. These institutions must fill a need and do it better or they cannot exist. Through the years only the highest quality institutions have survived and that survival of the fittest has resulted in a strain of schools that are now increasingly attracting the attention of policymakers, leaders of business and industry, the public, students and parents.

While seemingly at a great disadvantage, private career schools are blessed with the inherent strengths that grow out of the necessity to be enterprising and competitive. Thus, they are examples of private initiative and entrepreneurship at its best.

The seventy-fifth anniversary of the Association coincides with over 150 years of service to the nation by these private institutions. Certainly, then, these institutions and the Association that represents them have come of age at a fortuitous time for America. All of America, especially those of us associated with private career school education, should be proud of the achievements of private career schools and thankful that they are ready to assume an even larger role in assuring the nation's future.

This book points with pride to our history and enlivens our spirit as we look to the future. I am proud of the role that the Association has played and even more optimistic about the future of it and its member institutions.

—JERRY W. MILLER

3

AICS at Work

Jim Phillips, Executive Director of the Accrediting Commission and Executive Vice President, chats informally with Jerry Miller, President of AICS.

Wendy Eager, Administrative Assistant, prepares a report.

AICS office staff works on schedules for accreditation visits, AICS correspondence, seminar materials, and much more.

Robert Guillen, Assistant Director of the
Accrediting Commission, goes over schedule with Michelle Michaelis, Assistant to
the President.

The Accrediting Commission meets to consider evaluation reports and to make deter-
minations on the accreditation status of private career schools applying for AICS
membership.

Robert Atwell, President of the American Council on Education, and Jerry Miller, sharing their mutual concerns about higher education.

Jerry Miller meets with Representative William Ford to discuss upcoming legislation affecting private career schools.

General Counsel Bill Clohan testifies before the Education and Labor Subcommittee.

Jim Phillips and Lou Klaric, Assistant Executive Director, meet with Marjorie Lenn, Director of Professional Services for COPA, to discuss accreditation matters.

Rhona Hartman, Director of HEATH, explains a telecommunications device for the deaf to Mary Wine, AICS Director of Professional Relations.

Jerry Miller looks over CPAT, an entry level skills assessment test, with Jacqueline Woods, Director of the ACT Washington Office.

Jack McCartan, Dean of AICS Management Institutes, reviews scheduled events with Mary Guffey, Director of Seminars and Institutes.

The Governmental Affairs Seminar gives members a chance to get up-to-date on Association activities.

Gretchen Treu, Coordinator of Seminars and Institutes, prepares for a faculty development workshop.

Larry Doyle, Director of Publications and Information, after checking some facts at the Library of Congress.

Mary Wine and Larry Doyle select photographs for AICS Compass.

Larry Doyle finalizes layout for AICS Compass.

AICS—Service Through Diversity

More than 1,100 AICS member schools and branch campuses operate in forty-six states, the District of Columbia, Guam, Cayman Islands, Puerto Rico, and Europe.

Schiller International University, Heidelberg, West Germany

Kensington Business Institute, Buffalo, New York

National Education Center, Sawyer Campus, Los Angeles, California

Brooks Institute, Santa Barbara, California

Cannon's International Junior College of Business of Honolulu, Honolulu, Hawaii

Huertas Junior College, Caguas, Puerto Rico

South College, Savannah, Georgia

Johnson & Wales College, Providence, Rhode Island

Northeast Institute of Education, Scranton, Pennsylvania

Krissler Business Institute, Poughkeepsie, New York

Stevens-Henager College of Business, Ogden, Utah

Schiller International University, Strasbourg, France

Business Education Institute, West Springfield, Massachusetts

Barnes Business College, Denver, Colorado

Schiller International
University, Paris, France

San Diego Golf Academy, Rancho Santa
Fe, California

International Business College, Fort
Wayne, Indiana

Jamestown Business College, Jamestown,
New York

Schiller International University, Wickham Court Campus, London, England

Hagerstown Business College, Hagerstown, Maryland

Sullivan Junior College of Business, Louisville, Kentucky

Electronic Data Processing College, Hato Rey, Puerto Rico

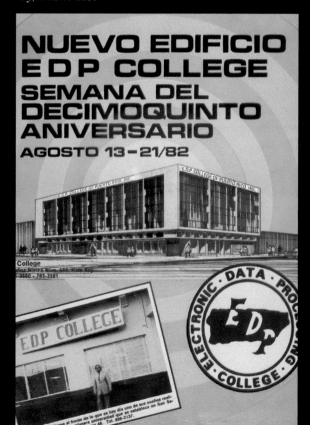

AICS—Students in Action

AICS schools and colleges are independent career-oriented institutions providing quality education designed to meet the job-related needs of students and employers. Our schools offer programs in over seventy fields.

Bookkeeping

Data processing

Filing

Dictaphone

Switchboard

Secretarial science

Paralegal

Word processing

Radio broadcasting

Photography

Offset printing

Drafting

Computer-aided design

Commercial art

Modeling

Merchandising

Fashion design

Retailing

Travel and tourism

Floral design

Culinary arts

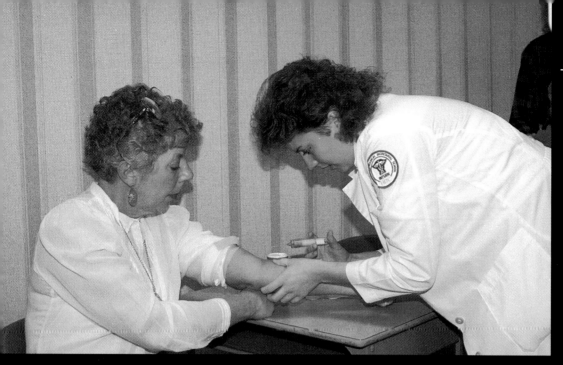

Phlebotomist

Medical lab technician

EKG technician

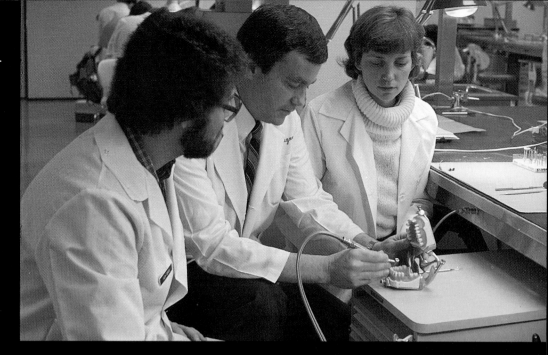

Dental lab technician

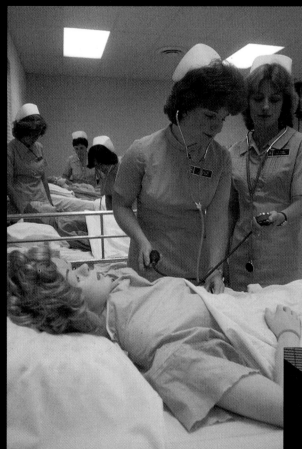

Practical nurse

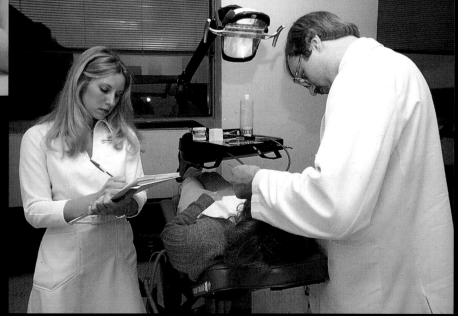

Dental office assistant

Surveying

Bank telle

Welding

Childcare specialist

Accounting

Introduction

Let's Celebrate

Throughout this year of 1987, we at the Association of Independent Colleges and Schools (AICS) have been joyously celebrating the organization's seventy-fifth anniversary. And we have good cause to celebrate because after three-quarters of a century, we continue to grow larger and stronger and to provide more and better services to our member institutions.

Our member schools currently have an estimated 718,000 students enrolled at more than 1,100 campuses and branches operating in forty-six states, the District of Columbia, Guam, the Cayman Islands, Puerto Rico, London, Paris, Madrid, Heidelberg, and Strasbourg. Enrollment at these schools has been climbing by as much as 15 to 20 percent each year as more and more students are attracted to the high-quality, career-specific educational programs our member schools provide.

For the past seventy-five years it has been the job of AICS to ensure that member schools maintain high academic standards and meet the needs of an ever-changing economy. It has also been our job to inform the public about our organization and its members, and to advise the nation's policymakers and lawmakers of the interests and needs of AICS member schools. We believe that we have fulfilled these mandates to the best of our ability and to the lasting benefit of our members.

Throughout our history, we have pursued an unrelenting quest for quality by maintaining the highest accreditation standards for our members. During the 1985-86 school year, AICS's hardworking Accrediting Commission met for a total of fifteen days and acted on 550 requests for accreditation or for changes in accreditation status. In addition, the Commission's dedicated staff accompanied evaluation teams to some four hundred school sites and processed thousands of pages of correspondence and documents to carry out the Commission's work.

Our quest for quality is also apparent in the dozens of professional development seminars and events we offer each year to the faculty and staff of AICS member schools. Every year, thousands of people attend

The annual Governmental Affairs Seminar provides AICS members with the opportunity to learn what is happening on Capitol Hill affecting their students.

In 1986 Jerry Miller and Bill Clohan presented the Distinguished Governmental Service Award to Congressman Mario Biaggi.

these seminars, which cover such topics as basic-skills instruction, management training, admissions management, financial aid, and student recruitment.

In recent years, AICS has achieved an overwhelming majority of its legislative goals. We have strengthened the Association's role at the state level so that it can effectively work with legislators for more equitable treatment of AICS students by state governments. We have established a political action committee to raise funds for candidates who support progressive higher-education legislation. And we have launched a systematic research program to identify the strengths and needs of private career schools and colleges so that we can better serve our members.

All of the work, throughout AICS's existence, has been aimed at making our member institutions an essential and respected component of postsecondary education. We believe we have achieved, and perhaps even surpassed, that goal. Students at our independent colleges and schools can prepare themselves for more than seventy careers. Member schools are dedicated to providing their students with hands-on, intensified training through professionally skilled faculty and the latest state-of-the-art equipment. The programs at these schools reflect areas of high employment growth, enabling graduates to enter the job market earlier than their counterparts from traditional public colleges. In addition, private career schools can respond more quickly to changes in the job market, helping students to acquire marketable skills, even in the midst of rapidly changing conditions.

AICS has helped make its member institutions a national educational resource. The United States Department of Education estimates that private career schools educate three out of four vocational students. These private schools depend totally on tuition and scholarship revenue to survive, yet they continue to thrive alongside public vocational schools that receive some $10 billion in federal and state aid each year. In addition, while public schools are tax-exempt, private career schools and colleges pay local, state, and federal taxes, and our member institutions maintain buildings and equipment that would cost taxpayers billions of dollars to duplicate. They save taxpayers more than $3,400 per student in tax subsidies each year, and, most importantly, they turn out graduates whose training and skills enable them to become taxpaying instead of tax-dependent citizens.

Now, as we come to the end of our seventy-fifth year, we at the Association of Independent Colleges and Schools are bursting with pride over these accomplishments. Of course, we are aware that there is still much more to be done, and we intend to keep striving not only to maintain the progress we have made in the past but to go on to higher achievements in the future. In the pages that follow we will tell you more about who we are and what we do.

Highly motivated students learn job-specific skills at AICS institutions.

Board of Directors, AICS

Chapter 1

The Mission

Since 1912, the Association of Independent Colleges and Schools has had one principal mission: to establish and advance the quality of education and the standards of excellence at private career schools and colleges. AICS serves students, member institutions, higher education, and society by striving to ensure academic excellence and ethical standards. To achieve these goals, the Association enforces strict accreditation criteria and procedures and supplies varied services to member institutions.

AICS members are independent, career-oriented institutions geared toward providing quality education, job training, and job placement to their students. They are committed to providing the educational opportunities and skills that today's employers demand. To achieve this end, each institution works to develop an understanding of local business and industry needs, and to design appropriate educational programs to fill those needs. The strong bond between the business community and career educators has led many schools to formalize their relationships with local industry by creating joint advisory boards. These boards help keep schools in touch with business developments, and result in better placement opportunities for graduates.

AICS institutions offer job-specific courses of study in more than seventy different fields, including accounting, secretarial science, drafting, computer science, fashion, allied health, and word processing. Depending on the institution, students who complete the course of study earn a diploma or certificate in a specific field, an associate's degree, a bachelor's degree, or, in some cases, a graduate-level degree. Enrollment at AICS member schools has increased 15 to 20 percent annually for the last several years and is expected to continue to grow steadily as employers increasingly demand the job-related educational skills that AICS institutions provide.

Since AICS institutions are largely dependent on tuition revenue, they stay in business by being responsive to the consumer's need for

In this age of rapidly growing technology, AICS institutions continue to offer job-specific programs to their students.

career education programs. Being consumer-responsive is a great advantage—it ensures that AICS institutions provide high-quality, relevant programs to serve the nation's businesses, industries, and nonprofit organizations.

KEEPING PACE WITH CHANGE

Because they are backed by private capital and fueled by private initiative, AICS institutions are better able to meet rapidly changing needs. Our competitive edge comes from the ability to remain flexible and responsive to change. The job-specific education that these institutions offer will become even more vital and will generate more demand as change accelerates in this age of technology and information. The Association's role is to help its member institutions keep pace with these rapid changes.

HOME BASE

The AICS headquarters are located in the impressive National Center for Higher Education building on Dupont Circle in Washington, D.C. Here we work among many of the most important organizations serving higher education in the United States. Among these are the American Council on Education, the Council on Postsecondary Accreditation, and the American Association of Collegiate Registrars and Admissions Officers. AICS headquarters are a short ride to Capitol Hill and to most of the administrative offices of the federal government.

MEMBERSHIP AND ORGANIZATION

There are three types of membership within AICS:

- *Member.* A member is any educational institution that offers programs in private career education and is accredited by the Accrediting Commission of AICS.

Doug Conner, Executive Director of AACRAO, and Jerry Miller discuss transfer of credit agreements.

AICS schools provide students with a realistic introduction to their chosen fields.

Clerical

Fashion merchandising and retailing

Dental lab technician

Library facilities are one of the areas examined when a school applies for accreditation.

- *Associate Member.* If an institution is not accredited by AICS, it may become an associate member if it is accredited by another national accrediting agency recognized by the United States Secretary of Education or by the Council on Postsecondary Accreditation. Associate members are admitted by a majority vote of the Board of Directors.

- *Allied Member.* An allied member is any person, firm, or corporation engaged in a trade, business, or profession related to the private career-education industry. Allied members are chosen by a majority vote of the Board of Directors.

Members elect the majority of the Board of Directors and Commissioners at the annual meeting of the Association. The Board of Directors, under the leadership of the chairman, is responsible for setting policy and communicating with staff. The Accrediting Commission establishes accreditation criteria and decides the accreditation status of member schools.

The Board employs the president of the Association, and the Accrediting Commission selects its executive director. The latter also serves as the executive vice president of the Association. These executives, and a staff of approximately twenty-five, carry out the daily operations of the Association. The staff oversee the areas of professional relations, educational programs, publications and information, and the Resource Center for State Affairs.

ACCREDITATION— OUR PREMIER SERVICE

The Association of Independent Colleges and Schools provides many different services to its members, but its primary function is accreditation. This is viewed as the single most important activity for promoting and maintaining quality in the delivery of educational services. The Accrediting Commission of the Association functions as an independent entity within the framework of the organization.

Controller Shelley Mitek checks the figures before presenting a report to the Budget and Finance Committee.

An institution must be accredited by the AICS Accrediting Commission before it can qualify for membership in the Association. Educational institutions offering programs of study in business-related private career education at the postsecondary level may apply for accreditation from AICS. The Commission is nationally recognized by the United States Secretary of Education and the Council on Postsecondary Accreditation. Other institutions may qualify for associate membership and full Association services if they are accredited by similarly recognized agencies.

Each member college or school earns its accreditation by meeting or exceeding a rigorous set of criteria. The nongovernmental accreditation that AICS and its fellow agencies provide is the most effective way to maintain standards and improve quality in postsecondary education. Employers require professional, comprehensive, and progressive training, and they regard accreditation as the principal assurance that the prospective employees have received quality education in the skills they need. In addition to serving as a hallmark of institutional quality, accreditation also provides AICS members with a systematic consultative process for improving quality.

The Accrediting Commission scrutinizes all phases of an institution's operations. Some of these areas include objectives of training, curriculum, administrative policy, teaching methods and materials, school plant and equipment, and library facilities. The Commission also examines student services, recruitment, guidance, placement, financial aid, follow-up, and students' records. In addition, the Commission investigates initially and monitors continuously the financial condition of any school applying for accreditation. The Association views accreditation as an ongoing process, not as a one-time-only initiation requirement. AICS expects its members not only to conform to accreditation standards but also to continually strive to surpass them.

Members of the Accrediting Commission at their annual meeting.

John T. South, III (left), President of South College, and Eleanor P. Vreeland, President of Katharine Gibbs Schools, Inc., discuss upcoming legislation with Congressman Pat Williams, Chairman of the House Subcommittee on Postsecondary Education.

Bonnie Voyles, Executive Vice President of Branell College, testifying before the Senate Subcommittee on Employment and Productivity. Voyles spoke on the benefits to students of the Job Training Partnership Act Amendments of 1986.

OTHER KEY SERVICES

Although accreditation is the primary service to members, AICS provides several other important services. Many are designed for the faculty and staff and ultimately benefit the students. Through its lobbying, fund-raising, and public-relations efforts, the Association informs the public and lawmakers of the interests and needs of AICS members.

Government Relations

The Association recognizes that national policymakers play a crucial role in gaining fair and equitable treatment for students in AICS institutions. AICS seeks out these policymakers and keeps them informed of the needs of member institutions and their students. At the national level, this means, in addition to working closely with members of both houses of Congress and their staff, conferring with top officials in key executive branch departments and agencies.

The Association's close relationships with the Congress and governmental agencies allow it to alert member institutions to legislation and regulations under consideration which could affect their students and their schools. AICS members and officers regularly offer testimony before congressional committees on issues affecting higher education. Through the years, AICS has earned a reputation as an authoritative and reliable representative for private career schools and colleges.

At the state level, the Association, together with the National Association of Trade and Technical Schools, supports a National Resource Center for State Affairs to provide services to strengthen state and regional associations of private career schools and to improve the government's understanding of the role of private career schools and colleges. Although much remains to be accomplished, AICS has made great strides in informing policymakers about the importance of career education.

Representation with Other Sectors of Higher Education

Because the Association is located in Washington, D.C., and housed in the National Center for Higher Education, it is an integral part of the multi-association structure serving all sectors of higher education in the United States. AICS is proud of its track record in communicating and cooperating with similar institutions committed to serving the needs of the higher education community. For example, the Association has coordinated an effort to act jointly on national issues with the American Vocational Association and the National Business Education Association through the AICS/AVA/NBEA Education for Business Coordinating Council.

AICS schools have traditionally emphasized education and training geared to employment opportunities.

Workshops, Seminars, and Institutes

The Association organizes and conducts workshops, seminars, and other programs on topics of importance to career educators. The Accrediting Commission is also extensively engaged in providing similar services to institutions seeking accreditation and to evaluators desiring to learn more about the institutional evaluation process. The participants in these programs benefit from ideas tested at other member schools, gain valuable training, and learn the latest techniques in such areas as managing a classroom, placing graduates, making the admissions process more efficient, and working with lawmakers to bring about favorable legislation.

Publications

Publications are a vital part of the AICS communications network. The Association produces a variety of publications to meet the diverse needs of its members. Probably the best known of these is the monthly newsletter, *AICS Compass*, which keeps members

Faculty Development Workshop
Improving Admissions Representative Effectiveness
AICS/NATTS State Association Meeting
Multiple Management Training Workshop
Establishing a Telemarketing Control Center and a Computerized System for Successful Admissions Management
Financial Aid for the Beginner
Placement Management
Tri-Management Training Workshops
How to Manage These Key Areas to Make Your School More Successful: Staff Selection, Training, Compensation, Team Building
Lead Festival—How to Develop More/Better Leads in the Face of a Declining Prospect Pool
How To Use Job Search Techniques To Improve Placement Success
Advanced Financial Aid
Are Senior Colleges Really Different?
Governmental Affairs Seminar
Teaching Office Technology
Management Program for School Directors

informed of Association activities, educational seminars, programs and activities of member schools and regional associations, and governmental actions.

In addition, there is *Capitol Comments*, a semimonthly newsletter, about federal activities affecting students and schools. The Association also offers specially developed publications that provide in-depth looks at public relations, advertising, and employee relations. Finally, the Association provides the administration and faculty at AICS schools with brochures on career opportunities, manuals on planning and development, directories, handbooks, and materials on accreditation criteria and procedures.

Research

The Association is involved with research concerning private colleges and schools and their students. In recent years, AICS has sponsored studies on student assistance, the role of private career colleges and schools and their students, and the impact of AICS institutions and their students on the nation's economy. The Association also sponsors the Dana R. Hart Memorial Research Grant, underwritten by the South-Western Publishing Company. The award is made annually to encourage research contributions in the field of private business education.

Quest for Quality

The quest for quality has become a consistent theme in the Association's programs. Increasingly, the Association is evaluating its activities in terms of whether they are effective in assisting member institutions and in delivering higher-quality instructional programs and student services, while at the same time engendering a creative, entrepreneurial spirit.

The Association pursues the quest for quality in a number of different ways. One of these is through a carefully planned and executed program of professional development. The As-

AICS educational programs such as the Management Institute offer a wide variety of workshops and seminars to members. These programs feature topics of interest to career educators and administrators.

38

sociation's Management Institute offers training workshops and conferences for members. One of these workshops, the AICS Management Program for School Directors, provides intensive leadership and skills development for individuals who have recently become, or are about to become, school directors. Since 1985, when the program began, over seventy-three people have successfully completed the course. AICS recognized early that competent and effective faculty and staff were the key factors in the drive for high-quality education. Thus, in the past year, we have expanded the number of professional development opportunities available to member schools. Nearly 2,700 participants from AICS schools attended thirty-six Association-sponsored events. Over 1,900 persons participated in AICS seminars, and another 950 registered for the annual meeting. Over the past year, more than five hundred schools purchased a faculty development package consisting of a videotape, a user's manual, and the popular *Students Come First* monograph concerning the needs of students.

The Xerox Center for Training and Management Development in Leesburg, Virginia, was the site of the 1986 AICS Management Program for School Directors.

Student Assessment

Another key factor in the quest for quality is student assessment, both at entry level and upon graduation. We need to determine what students know when they begin a course of study at a member school and what they have learned when they have completed the course of study. In response to what we believe is a strong national push to assess learning outcomes, the Association has joined forces with a major national test developer. Together we will develop interinstitutional entrance and outcome tests to measure the productivity of our member schools.

The quest for quality also includes a commitment to basic-skills instruction. All but the most selective colleges and universities are having to face up to the problem that they are enrolling students with serious deficiencies in the basic academic skills, the building blocks of learning. For AICS institutions, basic skills present

Assessing needs and setting realistic goals are part of our continuing quest for quality.

both a problem and an opportunity. To meet this challenge, the Association has begun developing plans to help AICS schools become more proficient and cost-effective in remediating basic skills and in developing programs to prepare students without high school diplomas to take the Graduate Equivalency Diploma (GED) test.

The quest for quality applies also to accreditation. The activities of the Accrediting Commission always have been directed at quality concerns, and members take pride in the growing recognition that the AICS Accrediting Commission is a leader among the nation's accrediting agencies. At this juncture, the Association has targeted faculty and staff development, student assessment, improved instruction in basic skills, and continued attention to improving accreditation as those areas that are most likely to help fulfill the quest for quality.

Mary Wine meets with Dan Lau, Director of Student Financial Aid Programs for the United States Department of Education, to discuss ways to minimize student loan defaults.

OUTREACH ACTIVITIES

The Association's major thrust in outreach activities is its involvement with state and federal legislatures and agencies. AICS has commented on several proposed regulations and has been successful in reducing the negative impact of proposed verification requirements for student loans. The Association also has taken affirmative steps to reduce loan default rates among private career-school and college students. This includes coordination with loan guarantors and lenders on a default prevention program and initiation of an institution-based program to prevent defaults. Finally, AICS recently filed an amicus brief in a state court action to challenge discriminatory practices in that state's student grant program.

As previously mentioned, the Association joined with the National Association of Trade and Technical Schools during 1985-86 to launch the NATTS/AICS Resource Center for State Affairs. The main objective of the Resource Center is to assist state associations of private career schools and colleges to attain their legislative and public-relations goals. Both associations feel this joint effort has been

The Grove Park Inn, site of the 1987 AICS Governmental Affairs Seminar. This annual event gives members an opportunity to make their concerns known to key congressional and federal officials.

an effective, cost-efficient means of assisting member institutions on the state level.

Another important way that the Association is helping to shape national policy is by the establishment of the Association of Independent Colleges and Schools Political Action Committee (AICSPAC). During its first year, AICSPAC raised almost $75,000 and contributed nearly $54,000 to candidates for federal offices who supported progressive higher-education legislation. This legislation included measures to provide equitable treatment of AICS students and to give students greater access to post-secondary-education institutions.

THE LONG-TERM AGENDA

The long-term and general goals of AICS are developed by the Board of Directors, the Accrediting Commission, and the Long-Range Planning Committee. The Long-Range Planning Committee advises the Board and the Commission on the need to develop appropriate plans to help the Association reach its goals and objectives. The Committee's major responsibility is to provide the Board periodically with a specific list of goals and objectives for its consideration.

The Association's agenda for the near future is complex, but it can be summarized as follows: AICS will continue to promote effective relationships at the federal level, and it will continue to improve the relationships between member institutions and governmental agencies on the state and local levels. It will seek to enhance the quality of member schools by assisting them with student assessment, faculty development, and remediation of basic skills. It will also

Meeting of the AICS Board of Directors.

continue to improve the accreditation process and help students gain access to financial aid. Achieving this agenda depends on every member school's full and active participation in the Association's many programs and activities.

MEMBERSHIP INVOLVEMENT

The dedication and commitment of member volunteers is the critical ingredient in helping the Association achieve its goals. The tasks are too great for any staff to accomplish alone, and it is only through the efforts of volunteers that the agenda can be planned and successfully implemented. In addition to the members who serve on the Board, the Commission, and the several committees cited previously, many members serve on the other standing committees of the Association and the Accrediting Commission.

Standing Committees of the Association

- The Academic Affairs and Faculty Development Committee determines activities that the Association can conduct for member institutions to help them improve their instructional programs and services, including curriculum matters and faculty development.
- The Awards and Recognition Committee determines who shall receive awards or other forms of recognition for distinguished service to the Association. The Board of Directors determines which awards or other recognition for distinguished service are to be given, but the selection of the recipient is the sole responsibility of the committee.
- The Education Articulation Committee is responsible for evaluating any situation that occurs which denies a member institution, a graduate of a member institution, or the Association itself appropriate recognition of its accrediting process. The committee recommends courses of action to overcome problems in

Meeting of the Finance and Budget Committee.

areas such as credit transfer, employment-reimbursement programs, general-directory listings, and access to certifying or licensing exams.

- The Finance and Budget Committee assists the treasurer in preparing the budget for presentation to the Board prior to the annual membership meeting. The committee also develops plans for raising funds for current and future needs.
- The Financial Aid Funding Committee advises the Board on policy positions the Association should take regarding the ability of member institutions to participate in a wide range of financial-assistance programs. The committee also has the responsibility of developing, if needed, alternative sources of student financial assistance.
- The Government Relations Committee advises the Board on actions or positions to take regarding laws and regulations that have been enacted or proposed by federal and state governments.
- The Information Resource Management Committee is charged with planning the utilization of technical equipment and personnel in managing the information needs of the Association's membership.
- The Management Education Committee plans workshops, seminars, and other educational presentations sponsored by the Association. It also supervises and reviews development of printed manuals on a variety of subjects of importance to the management of independent institutions.
- The Memorabilia Committee identifies and collects materials related to the history of the Association and its predecessor groups. In addition, the committee collects literature detailing the history of private career schools and colleges so that it may be preserved in the Association library.
- The Public Relations Committee plans effective strategies for all Association public-relations projects and materials and advises the president on the appropriateness of the approach and language of AICS news releases and publications.

Senator Claiborne Pell (left), and Dr. George Petrello, member of the AICS Accrediting Commission, during a visit to Bryant College.

- The Research Committee develops plans for research activities to be conducted by the Association or by the Foundation for the Advancement of Vocational Occupational Research. The committee provides the organization with research projects that will further AICS objectives.
- The Student Financial Aid Administration Committee serves as an advisory group on matters pertaining to the administration of student financial aid in member institutions.
- The Veterans Affairs and Military Education Committee advises the Board on matters pertaining to the Veterans Administration regulations and requirements and identifies ways in which AICS institutions can be of greater service to military personnel on active duty, serving in the military forces, or serving in the National Guard.

Standing Councils and Committees of the Accrediting Commission

The Commission has three councils that deliberate on all policies and matters related to the accrediting process. These three councils are the Council on Schools, the Council on Colleges, and the Council on Research and Service. Four committees aid the Commission in its work.

AICS institutions offer courses in over 70 fields of study.

Designing for exhibits

Commercial art

Court reporting

- The Criteria Review Committee reviews the accreditation criteria and recommends revisions to the Commission. In doing so, the committee publishes proposed criteria revisions for membership review, and considers any comments it may receive about the proposed changes.
- The Education Review Committee reviews all aspects of the educational activities of member institutions, including the development of the evaluative processes required by the Commission.
- The Evaluation Review Committee reviews and revises the Commission's procedures for evaluating schools. The committee is concerned with the training of evaluators, team-report formats, and the length of on-site visits.
- The Financial Review Committee monitors the annual financial statements of institutions and recommends policies and procedures for managing the Commission's finances.

A LONG LOOK BACK

Now that we have told you who we are, what we stand for, and what we do, we will next take a look at the history of the Association of Independent Colleges and Schools. We will describe how we arrived at this Diamond Jubilee on a journey back through our silver and golden years. We will also take you back beyond 1912 to recall the proud past of private career education.

Travel and tourism

Merchandising

Broadcasting

Chapter 2
Genesis and Roots

As America developed from a group of tiny agricultural colonies to one of the world's great industrial nations, private career education kept pace, growing steadily from one single tutor in Plymouth Colony to a great modern network of independent schools and colleges. From its earliest years, whenever America's expanding industry and commerce required trained workers, private vocational schools always met those needs first and best. As you will see in this chapter, this ability to respond quickly to the ever-changing educational needs of society has remained an inherent characteristic throughout the history of private career education.

What we now think of as office or business skills were first taught formally in Europe during the Renaissance. The earliest vocational teachers were tutors who taught students in their homes or who traveled from place to place teaching subjects such as arithmetic, penmanship, and early forms of accounting. Later, these subjects were taught in academies, schools, and universities. As Europeans began to settle in America, the same kinds of tutorial systems and schools developed here. These schools continued to grow and thrive because they were able to keep pace with the Industrial Revolution, and later with changing social conditions and office methods, as well as with the inventions of mechanical devices such as typewriters, telephones, steno machines, calculators, and computers.

HERITAGE

The earliest business subjects—accounting, arithmetic, and penmanship—were first taught by an Italian monk, Father Luca Pacioli (1445–1517). During his time, Venice had become one of the world's great trading centers. The city's merchants and bankers needed to learn how to use the Arabic numeral system, which was then beginning to replace the old Roman system, and they also needed a method to keep track of

From Chicago, I went to Albany, where on the first day of January, 1857, I started unaided what is now known as Albany Business College.

How well I remember the first student who took his seat in those rooms. How carefully I nurtured him; how tenderly I treated him. During all my teaching in subsequent days I doubt if any student ever had more faithful attention.

Gradually the number increased, and when I received my twenty-first student in the Albany Business College, I said the school was no longer an infant; and I invited the whole school to go out with me and eat ice cream; and we turned the key in the outside door while we did it.

Silas S. Packard

Silas S. Packard, 1826–1898, founder of Albany Business College and pioneer in independent career education.

their purchases and sales. To fill these needs, Pacioli wrote in 1494 *Summa de arithmetica*, a massive work that covered the general field of mathematics and included several charts of weights, measures, and money used in the Italian city-states. Equally important, the book also introduced the Italian method of double-entry bookkeeping that, in modern form, is still in use today.

The writings of Pacioli survived the test of time and were reformulated into *Debitor and Creditor*, a text authored by Hugh Oldcastle of London, in 1543. From that time, tutors routinely taught courses in accounts, arithmetic, and penmanship. The great European Age of Exploration led to the discovery of the New World and new trade routes to the Far East. These discoveries opened up new markets for European merchants and further increased the need for trained employees. Tutors began adding surveying and navigation to their other courses, and the instruction they provided enabled their students to move quickly into the job market. In effect, the early days of vocational education were the beginning of the era of "learn to earn."

These early vocational courses were taught not only in Europe but also in the American colonies long before the Revolutionary War. They also predate the first teachings of vocational subjects in American public schools by more than a century and a half. In fact, the very first private career education took place in the Plymouth Colony in 1635. In that year, the colony hired James Morton to teach reading, writing, and the casting of accounts to the children of New England. (The National Business Education Association defines "casting accounts" as a course in practical arithmetic. This would have included many of the topics covered today in a business math course.)

Although the hiring of Morton marked the beginning of vocational education in the American colonies, most people learned through an apprentice system. If someone wanted to become a bookkeeper or surveyor, he or she learned the skills on the job. This system was slow to change throughout the history of American vocational education and still exists today in some industrial trades.

PIONEER SCHOOLS AND THEIR LEADERS

Details of the first private schools devoted to training for business are unclear. However, we are certain that private schools were offering vocational or business education long before the nation's public education system was developed.

As New York and Boston became important trade centers in the colonies, the art of bookkeeping became formalized. It is probably safe to assume that tutors offered instruction in bookkeeping in these cities before 1700. We know for certain that John Green offered it in Boston in 1709, and George Brownell taught bookkeeping in New York in 1731. In 1729, Isaac Greenwood wrote the first arithmetic textbook, entitled *Arithmetick, Vulgar And Decimal; With The Applications Thereof To A Variety of Cases In Trade And Commerce.*

The first school to teach vocational subjects was probably the Academy of Philadelphia, founded by Benjamin Franklin in 1749. The academy, which later became the University of Pennsylvania, offered arithmetic, accounts, and the history of commerce, as well as French, German, and Spanish, to the area merchants. Franklin had wanted the academy to teach practical subjects, especially English, but gradually it became a classical school. It dropped English for Latin and lost interest in teaching vocational subjects.

As the colonies continued to grow, so did the scope of bookkeeping as an important discipline. In 1796 Benjamin Workman published *American Accountant*, the first textbook on bookkeeping. The English Classical School for Boys in Boston added bookkeeping to its curriculum in 1823. Four years later the Massachusetts legislature enacted a law requiring all municipalities of five hundred families or more to establish a high school. Part of the required curriculum in these schools was a course in bookkeeping.

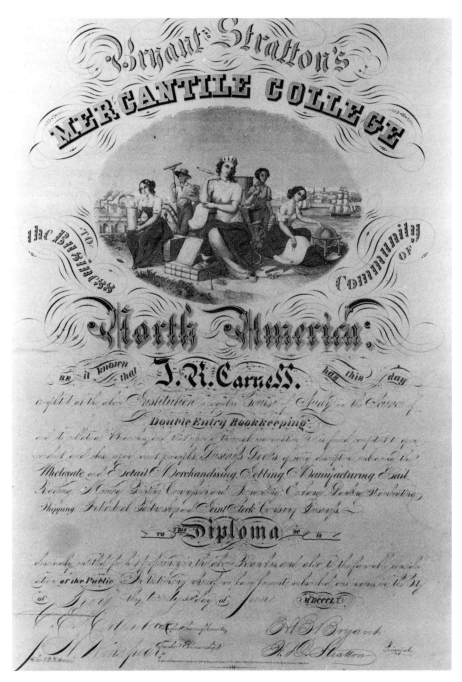

John R. Carnell's diploma from Bryant and Stratton's Mercantile College dated 1865. Carnell later purchased Albany Business College. ABC is still owned and operated by the Carnell family.

PRESIDENTS AND PRINCIPALS

1857	Silas S. Packard
1863	E. G. Folsom
1878	E. G. Folsom and C. E. Carhart
1884	John R. Carnell and C. E. Carhart
1888	John R. Carnell and S. D. Gutchess
1896	John R. Carnell and Benton S. Hoit
1920	Prentiss Carnell, John R. Carnell, Jr., Benton S. Hoit
1930	Prentiss Carnell, Sr.
1958	Prentiss Carnell, Jr.
1972	Prentiss Carnell III

The Turn of the Century

Child labor was first recognized as a social problem with the introduction of the factory system.

J. P. Morgan built the family fortune into a colossal financial and industrial empire. In 1901 he formed the U.S. Steel Corporation, the first billion-dollar corporation in the world.

Combined harvester and thrasher, circa 1910.

"Going up," cried the driver as he threw in the clutch of his Model T Roadster, and the little car began to climb the stairs of the YMCA building in Columbus, Nebraska.

With straw hat in hand, Henry Ford sits behind the wheel of a 1903 Model A.

On December 17, 1903, this airplane, invented by Orville and Wilbur Wright, rose for a few seconds to make the first heavier-than-air flight in history.

Early switchboard operators in Hamburg, New York.

Typical American office scene, circa 1900.

Physical fitness was always in style.

Suffragettes marching on Fifth Avenue in
New York City.

Worried women investors in broker's office
during the Wall Street Panic of 1901.

With tailcoats flailing, the Keystone Kops lurched past the camera and left us laughing.

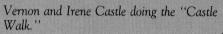

Vernon and Irene Castle doing the "Castle Walk."

The beautiful Ethel Barrymore at the beginning of her illustrious career.

The private career schools responded quickly to all of these changes in business methods, technology, and female employment. Curricula soon included instruction in shorthand and the operation of business machines such as the typewriter, calculator, and stenograph machine. In addition, private career education was developing in other ways. Several years before the Civil War, H. B. Stratton, a student of P. R. Spencer, teamed with Henry B. Bryant to establish their first school in Cleveland. By the mid-1860s, an estimated fifty schools were under their management. Bryant and Stratton were the initiators of standardized methods in school management and educational activities. They used uniform textbooks throughout the chain, and they held periodic management meetings at which they determined policies and methods to be applied to all of the schools in the chain.

Another of the well-known chains established in the late 1800s was the Draughon Schools located in the South and Midwest. John F. Draughon, the founder of these schools, began business in 1889 with an investment of $60. After the turn of the century, he owned forty-eight schools in eighteen states that were valued at more than $300,000. Draughon also operated a textbook company from which most of the texts for his schools were purchased. (This was probably the first example of vertical integration of management in the private school business.)

In 1862, the public sector of higher education entered the field of post-secondary vocational education. The Morrill Act, perhaps better known as the Land Grant Act, gave each state land that it could use in any way it chose. The proceeds from the land were to be used to establish "land grant" colleges to teach agriculture, mechanical arts, engineering, and military science. This act helped establish state university systems in Illinois, California, Minnesota, and Wisconsin. Many believed this legislation would be detrimental to private career schools, but that fear proved to be unfounded.

A typing class at Jacobs Business College in 1907. Jacobs later merged with Miami Commercial College to become the Miami-Jacobs Junior College.

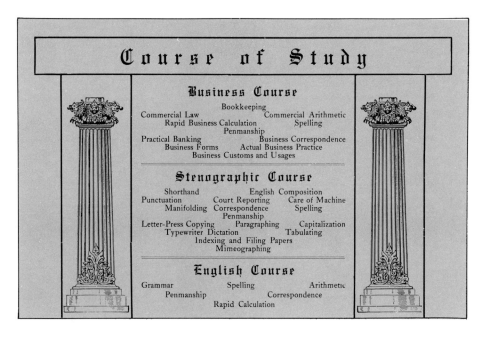

Reprinted from Jacobs Business College catalog, circa 1906.

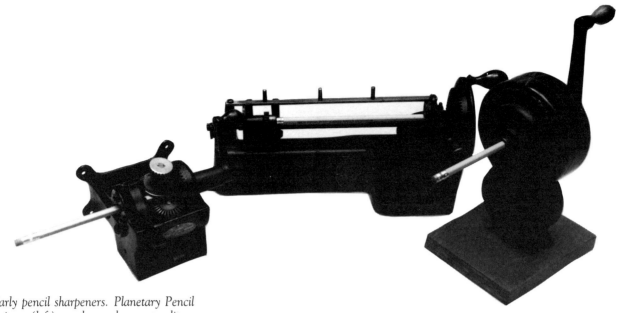

Early pencil sharpeners. Planetary Pencil Pointer (left) can be used as a standing or wall model.

INFANT ALLIANCES

The competition that marked the early history of private career education still exists today, but the industry has matured and become more sophisticated. Those in it have learned that, even within a competitive framework, sharing and cooperation are necessary for survival.

In the 1800s, owners could not foresee the mutual advantages of alliances necessary for building a common base for the private career industry. Instead, they practiced what one observer has called the fourth "R" of private career school educators—reticence. Therefore, strong professional associations were not formed until the twentieth century.

However, some alliances were formed that were similar to our current concept of franchising. In 1865, a number of the principals who owned interests in regional schools in the Bryant and Stratton chain seceded and organized the National Union of Business Colleges. Among those in the new organization were several of the most capable managers. Their independence, however, was short-lived. Concessions were made by the parent Bryant and Stratton organization, and, in 1866, they rejoined the fold, forming a new alliance. (The scenario was a kind of mini-Civil War in the industry at a very apropos time!)

The new alliance was known as the International Business College Association. In many ways, it replaced the old Bryant and Stratton organization, which had begun to deteriorate even before the death of Mr. Stratton in 1867. The alliance was formed around an agreement among the various member institutions to establish uniform minimum tuition rates and scholarships that were transferable from school to school.

In 1866, the International Business College Association held a convention in Cleveland. Private career schools were achieving such national prominence that *Harper's Weekly* devoted an entire page to a reproduction of pen-and-ink sketches of the members of the association.

NEW COMPETITION

In 1890, the first commercial high school in the United States was founded. The founding of Washington Commercial High School, in Washington, D.C., marked the beginning of a new type of competition for private career schools. Another commercial high school opened in Brooklyn in 1899, followed by one in New York City in 1901, and another in Boston in 1908. As competition from the public sector intensified, the old fears roused by the Land Grant Act of 1862 were revived and, once again, they proved unwarranted.

The Dictaphone, circa 1904.

The Junior, manufactured in 1907, was fully keyed yet compact enough to fit in an overcoat pocket. The manufacturer claimed it had a writing capacity of 80 words per minute.

FROM SEEDS TO ROOTS

The roots of the Association for Independent Colleges and Schools were set in place in 1912. Over a period of approximately seventy-five years, the private career school industry had finally developed. During the gestation period, the schools devoted themselves primarily to the disciplines of bookkeeping, accounting, business mathematics, penmanship, shorthand, typewriting, and machine calculating operations. In the beginning, the student population was largely male; but by the end of the nineteenth century, a growing percentage of females participated as private career school students, and later as office workers.

The public sector of vocational education gradually began to offer courses on the postsecondary and secondary levels in the same subject areas covered by the private schools. Although initially this activity appeared to be a serious threat to the private sector, it turned into an opportunity for the private schools to meet the individual instructional needs of students more efficiently and to develop better methods of placing graduates in skilled positions. Apparently the mission and strategy of the private career schools were on target. Their growth, in terms of the number of schools and student populations, paralleled the growth trend of the nation.

This historical overview points out one major shortcoming of the private career institutions in the nineteenth century. They failed to understand the need to band together for purposes of sharing ideas and developing an industry-wide image. (This could also be said for many other industries of that era.) Fortunately, the necessity to join together in a meaningful way was recognized early in the twentieth century.

Chapter 3

Going for the Silver (1912 – 1937)

$\mathbf{T}$he year is 1912. President Taft proclaims to the world that the United States owns the Panama Canal and can regulate the canal's tolls. Meanwhile, Woodrow Wilson, outgoing President of Princeton University, waits in the wings as President-elect of the United States. Ethel Barrymore is a sensation on Broadway in *The Witness for the Defense*. And "Alexander's Ragtime Band" and "You Great Big Beautiful Doll" are two of the hit songs of the year.

In Stockholm, inspired by the gifted athlete Jim Thorpe, the United States Olympic team earns the most points in overall competition. Statesman Elihu Root is awarded the Nobel Peace Prize, and Pablo Picasso completes one of his greatest paintings, *The Violin*. Back home, the Boston Red Sox capture the World Series.

This was truly a year to remember. On its maiden voyage from Southampton, England, to New York, the "unsinkable" *Titanic* hit an iceberg and sank to the ocean's bottom. New Mexico and Arizona were admitted to the Union as the forty-seventh and forty-eighth states, respectively, and several thousand miles away the emperor of China abdicated and a republic was established.

In this same year the National Association of Accredited Commercial Schools (NAACS) was founded.

FOUNDERS AND FOUNDATIONS

Chicago was stormier than usual on December 12, 1912. Yet the Christmas season was in full swing. At the request of Benjamin Franklin Williams, President of Capital City Commercial College of Des Moines, Iowa, twenty-two school administrators took time from their hectic schedules and came to Chicago for a meeting at the Hotel La Salle. At this meeting the twenty-three private career-school leaders entered into

Ben Williams, President of Capital City Commercial College and first President of NAACS.

H.E.V. Porter, President of Jamestown Business College and first Secretary of NAACS.

an enduring alliance that developed into the Association of Independent Colleges and Schools. Although their schools represented only a fraction of the 155,000 men and women studying in private business schools at the time, these men established the foundation of an association that would eventually have a tremendous impact on the private career sector.

The original mission of the National Association of Accredited Commercial Schools, as set forth by founder Ben Williams, was "to develop and maintain higher educational, business, and ethical standards in commercial education, and insofar as may be legal, proper and desirable, to protect the interest and enlarge the usefulness of member schools."

The twenty-three organizers signed their newly drafted charter, which read as follows:

We, the undersigned, representing the Commercial schools affixed after our names, do hereby make application for membership in the National Association of Accredited Commercial Schools and agree that if elected to membership in the organization we will conform to the rules of the Association and be governed by them, and will pay the fees as prescribed by the Constitution and By-Laws. This agreement shall be binding upon the schools whose names are affixed when one hundred schools have been accepted and enrolled, at which time $25.00, one-fourth of the annual fee, shall be paid into the Treasury.

Apparently the charter members were more anxious to get started than the charter indicated. The record shows that they immediately voted each other into membership, paid the $25.00 initial dues, and elected officers to serve on a governing board.

Williams was elected President of the Association—a title and responsibility that he held for twenty-five years. Hubert E. V. Porter, President of Jamestown Business College of Jamestown, New York, was elected Secretary. The history of the organization indicates that this was a very important position and one he served faithfully for many years. D. C. Rugg, of Minneapolis Business College in Minnesota, became the first Treasurer of the organization. It was obvious that custodial duties would not be burdensome in this job. Vice presidents were elected from four regions of the country. Charles M. Miller, of the Miller School of Business in New York City, served as Eastern Division Vice President; Enos Spencer, of the Spencerian Commercial School in Louisville, Kentucky, served as Southern Division Vice President; H. B. Boyles, of Boyles Business College in Omaha, Nebraska, served as Central Division Vice President; and L. A. Arnold, of Central Business College in Denver, served as Western Division Vice President. All served as the directors of the Association.

Other charter members included:

- P. S. Spangler, Duff's College, Pittsburgh, Pennsylvania
- Morton MacCormac, MacCormac School, Chicago, Illinois
- W. B. Elliott, Elliott Commercial School, Wheeling, West Virginia
- Otis L. Trenary, College of Commerce, Kenosha, Wisconsin
- B. A. Munson (by proxy), Waukegan Business College, Waukegan, Illinois
- J. F. Fish, Northwestern Business College, Chicago, Illinois
- W. E. Harbottle, The Jacobs Business College, Dayton, Ohio
- W. N. Watson, Lincoln College, Lincoln, Nebraska
- W. W. Dale, Janesville Business College, Janesville, Wisconsin
- Almon F. Gates, Waterloo Business College, Waterloo, Iowa
- Victor Lee Dodson, Wilkes-Barre Business College, Wilkes-Barre, Pennsylvania
- J. R. Anderson, Barnes Business College, St. Louis, Missouri
- E. M. Johnston, The Elyria Business College, Elyria, Ohio
- M. M. Cassel, Erie Business College, Erie, Pennsylvania
- F. M. Allen, Hamilton Business College, Hamilton, Ohio
- D. D. Miller, Miller School of Business, Cincinnati, Ohio

Although "accredited" appeared in the name of the Association, it did not have the same meaning it has today. Accreditation in the NAACS sense referred to the acceptance of an institution's application for membership, although this meaning changed

Three generations at Miami-Jacobs Junior College. William E. Harbottle (pictured at the rear), son Charles P. Harbottle (seated), and grandson Charles G. Campbell.

1912–1937

American flying ace, Eddie Rickenbacker.

President Wilson asked Congress for a declaration of war on April 2, 1917.

V. I. Lenin addressing the masses.

French class at Fort Custer, Michigan.

Girl Scouts collected peach pits to burn and make into charcoal for gas-mask filters.

You Save Peach Seeds — They Will Save Soldiers Lives

The "unsinkable" goes down.

Clarence Darrow (left), attorney for the defense, and William Jennings Bryan, attorney for the prosecution—and prosecution witness—in the Scopes Trial in 1925.

Anxious investors wait on the steps of the sub-treasury building across the street from the New York Stock Exchange in October 1929.

Abandoned farmhouse in the Dust Bowl of Oklahoma.

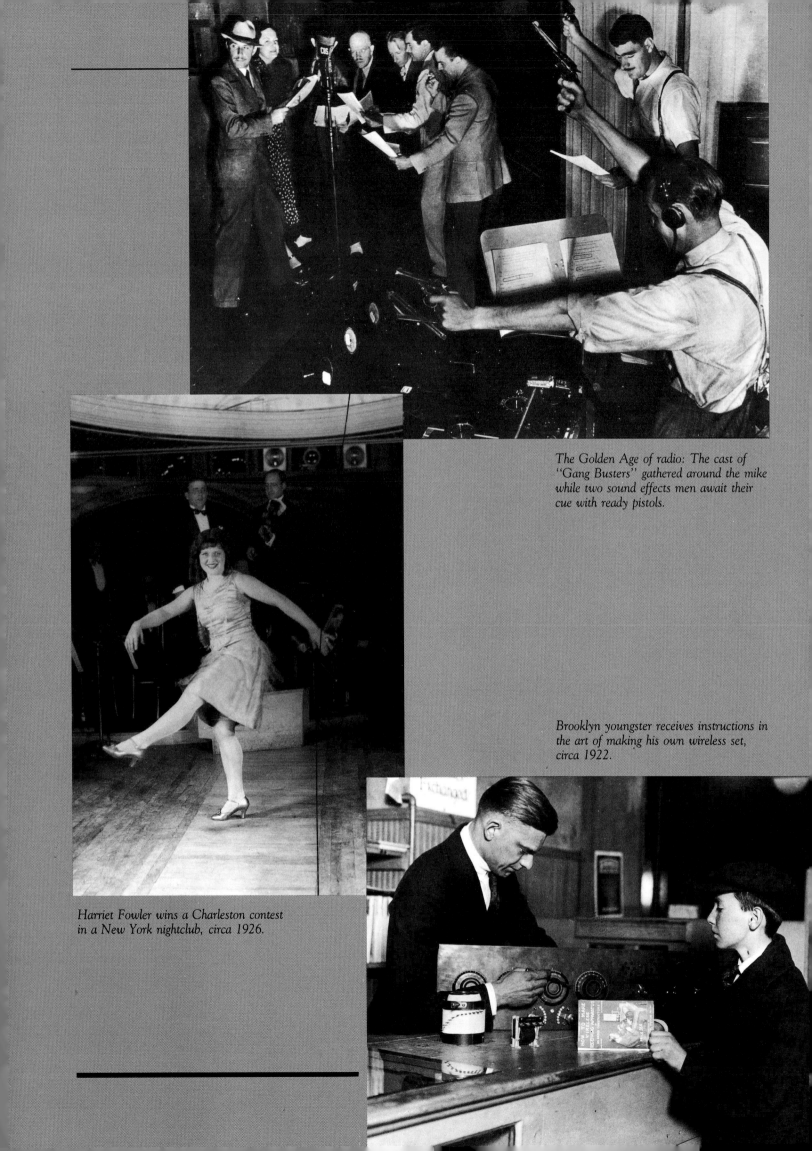

The Golden Age of radio: The cast of "Gang Busters" gathered around the mike while two sound effects men await their cue with ready pistols.

Brooklyn youngster receives instructions in the art of making his own wireless set, circa 1922.

Harriet Fowler wins a Charleston contest in a New York nightclub, circa 1926.

Mickey Mouse arrives on the screen in 1928 as the hero of "Steamboat Willie."

A Shirley Temple look-alike contest.

The romantic star of American silent motion pictures, Rudolph Valentino.

Switchboard operator, circa 1922.

later. When we look back at all aspects of education in the early 1900s, we note that accreditation as a formal process was in its very earliest stages, and few true accrediting agencies existed.

HISTORICAL ENVIRONMENT

Major historical events occurred both within and outside the environment of vocational education during the first twenty-five years of NAACS' existence. World events, including those that involved the United States, were a "mixed bag" from 1912 through 1937.

The United States emerged from the Victorian Age as an industrial and agricultural giant. A spirit of optimism backed up by large doses of economic growth and development prevailed. The great temples of commerce, such as the Empire State Building in New York City and the Wrigley Building in Chicago, provided physical evidence of the prosperity of the times. Management philosophy and practice took on the flavor of a discipline, and the vocational arts and sciences thrived.

World War I created great trauma at home and abroad. Nevertheless, the United States came out of the war victorious and invigorated. There was hope of a lasting peace with the formation of the League of Nations. Then, after a period of economic growth and financial successes, the world shook again with bad news as the Stock Market crashed in 1929. The economic news remained bad for almost a decade.

Major events were happening in vocational education as well. In 1911, shortly before the establishment of the NAACS, Frederick W. Taylor, considered by many the "father of scientific management," wrote the first textbook on the subject. The work was the culmination of Taylor's research and published articles on making the workplace more efficient and effective.

The NAACS faced strong and increasing competition from the public sector in the early years. In 1915, just after the formation of NAACS, the National Education Association appointed a committee to develop business curricula for public high schools. In 1917, the Smith-Hughes Act made federal funds available to schools that provided business training on a part-time basis to employed individuals. And in 1937, the George-Dean Act was passed, allotting funds to teachers, supervisors, and teacher trainers in the area of distributive education. These actions in the public sector of vocational education created formidable challenges to private career schools.

Associations and publications related to career education proliferated between 1912 and 1937. The American Assembly of Collegiate Schools of Business was founded in 1916, and the National Association of Office Managers in 1919. The American Vocational Association was established in 1926, and the American Business Communication Association in 1935. Influenced by the work of Frederick W. Taylor, William Leffingwell, a pioneer in office-management techniques, wrote the first office-management book in 1917. The South-Western Publishing Company, an outgrowth of the Knoxville Business College, began publication of a professional journal called *The Balance Sheet* in 1919. And in 1920, *The American Shorthand Teacher*, another publication for professionals, was first published by the Gregg Publishing Company.

Technological progress also increased rapidly during the first twenty-five years of NAACS. Electricity became generally available and revolutionized the way people lived and worked. Radio linked all parts of the nation together in a network of instant communication. Railroads and automobiles made travel faster and more practical. Automatic calculating machines, mechanically improved typewriters, recording machines, and telephones improved office procedures.

THE EARLY YEARS

The growth of the NAACS was slow during the first two years. After 1914, however, membership increased rap-

Miss Rosa Fritz, for years champion typist of the world, visited the Roanoke Business College in January, and made the statement that, not only is the college building and the course of study and the Faculty equal to any in the country and superior to most of them, but that the Typewriting Department, in particular, is deserving of special mention for the high-grade character of its work.

—Roanoke National Business College catalog, 1913

Typing class at Jacobs Business College, circa 1913.

73

The banner of the International Business College.

idly under the aggressive leadership of W. N. Watson, Chairman of the Membership Committee. In those days, an applicant was admitted to membership by the Board of Governors after the proprietor of the school had filed a lengthy application. This application had to be supported by recommendations furnished by the other private career-school owners, local bankers, and public-school officials.

In addition to the Membership Committee, several other committees were formed within the framework of the Association. One of the most important was the Educational Committee. W. B. Elliott, proprietor of the Elliott Commercial School of Wheeling, West Virginia, was the head of the Educational Committee during the 1920s and 1930s. Under Elliott's leadership, model programs in shorthand, typewriting, and bookkeeping were developed. The Educational Committee also served as liaison with the North Central Association of Colleges and Secondary Schools and the United States Bureau of Education. (The North Central Association is the agency that grants accreditation to universities and secondary schools in the north-central states.)

The Vigilance Committee was another important committee established during the early years. J. L. Harmon, President of Bowling Green Business University of Bowling Green, Kentucky, was the first head of the Vigilance Committee. This committee closely resembled a modern ac-

creditation group since it was responsible for ensuring that the membership complied with the code of ethics regarding business practices and educational policies. The committee dealt with complaints and visited member schools from time to time. Several years after the formation of the Vigilance Committee, its name was changed to the Better Business Bureau (which should not be confused with the association that bears that name today).

For many years, the National Association of Accredited Commercial Schools had neither a full-time staff nor facilities of its own. Most of the work was done through the offices of the Association's president, Ben Williams, and secretary, Hubert Porter. As time went on, Porter's office became the center for communications.

During the Association's first twenty-five years, an annual convention was faithfully held sometime between Christmas Day and the start of the New Year. Most of these gatherings took place at the Sherman Hotel in Chicago. The meetings frequently concluded with a gala banquet in the Sherman's Crystal Ballroom. Prominent state and federal officials were invited to attend. Occasionally, annual meetings were held in other large cities on the main rail lines, such as Cleveland, Philadelphia, and Detroit. Similar to today's special airline fares for convention travelers were the reduced rail fares for members attending the annual meeting that were often obtained by the early convention organizers.

After almost five years of existence, the Association decided to become legally incorporated. It seems that the founding fathers may have been reluctant to take that step until they were confident the infant union would survive. Acting on behalf of the membership, the Board of Governors incorporated the NAACS on May 25, 1917, in the District of Columbia.

The entrepreneurial spirit of the membership surfaced with the establishment of the Accredited Schools Supply Company in 1917. Set up as a cooperative, this spinoff company's job was to furnish supplies and publish textbooks for the member schools. Members of the cooperative were able to purchase shares of stock in the new company. The Accredited Schools Supply Company published a typing manual, a two-volume penmanship textbook, a three-volume English course, and texts on spelling, arithmetic, and commercial law. The cooperative had a good record for paying dividends to the shareholders, but the Depression of the 1930s spelled doom for this operation.

The Association was successful in obtaining educational discounts for the membership from various typewriter manufacturers. It had discount arrangements with the Royal Typewriter Company, the Woodstock Typewriter Company, and, later, with the Remington, Underwood, and L. C. Smith companies. Members viewed these special rates as a major benefit of membership, especially during the Depression years.

ETHICS AND EDUCATIONAL POLICIES

The benefits of membership, for commercial schools struggling to survive and to thrive in a highly competitive environment, were a strong inducement to join the organization in the early days. An important benefit was the affiliation with a group that emphasized its members' adherence to a strict code of ethical practice in both educational management and the delivery of instructional services.

By the year 1920 all members were required to subscribe to a code of ethics and educational policies, which, as stated by the Association, included:

• Employ at all times an adequate number of good teachers and main-

Reprinted from Accredited News.

Banking and office department at Utica School of Commerce.

LEST WE FORGET

Ten Commandments not from Mt. Sinai, but from a large gathering of N. A. A. C. S. members assembled many years ago. Have we all kept the faith?

THOU SHALT NOT—

1. Guarantee positions.
2. Cut tuition rates.
3. Fail to pay thy debts.
4. Indulge in exaggeration or misrepresentation.
5. Attempt to entice students away from any other school.
6. Conduct thy business upon low levels.
7. Abuse thy competitor or thy fellow educator.
8. Dodge thy Association responsibilities.
9. Use "Accredited" without using also, "National Association of Accredited Commercial Schools."
10. In any manner, bring reproach upon thy calling.

Reprinted from Accredited News.

tain suitable quarters and equipment for the programs and community to be served.

• Pay legitimate debts promptly and in a businesslike manner.

• Deal honorably in all student-relation matters.

• Avoid exaggeration of every kind and form in advertising.

• Make no misleading statements or misrepresentations of any kind, either in person or through any agency.

• Cultivate within the school itself and in its community the highest possible moral standards.

• Refuse, either directly or indirectly, to guarantee positions to prospective students, and refrain from making statements regarding prospective employment that are not fully corroborated by the experience of the school.

• Report promptly to the proper officer of the Association any violation of the ethics of the profession, as understood by this Association, whether these violations occur within or without the membership of the Association.

• Submit disagreements among members to a Board of Arbitrators.

In addition, the code of ethics demanded that "Each member of this Association shall be one whose char-

ACCREDITED NEWS

OFFICIAL ORGAN OF THE NATIONAL ASSOCIATION OF ACCREDITED COMMERCIAL SCHOOLS

(COPYRIGHTED 1921)

Vol. 1 No. 1	JAMESTOWN, N. Y.	FEBRUARY, 1921

First issue of Accredited News.

acter and reputation are above reproach, and who shall so order his general conduct as to entitle him to be regarded as a suitable person to direct the education and moral development of the young people of his institution."

These rather straightforward edicts have withstood the test of time. Most of them remain as important to the Association today as they were in the early days. As the French proverb states, "Plus ça change, plus c'est la même chose" (The more things change, the more they stay the same).

COMMUNICATIONS

By February of 1921, the Association had grown from its 23 charter members to a grand total of 228 members. But as membership grew, so did the problem of internal communications. A solution to this problem was suggested at the Cleveland Convention in 1920, when the secretary of the Association, Hubert Porter, was called upon to publish a newsletter for the membership.

Published in Jamestown, New York, Volume 1, Number 1, of *Accredited News* appeared in February 1921. It was described as the "Official Organ of The National Association of Accredited Commercial Schools." Below its letterhead, and centered on the front page, was the Association's logo, referred to as "The Emblem of

The Oliver No. 5, list price $100, featured a special bottle of Oliver Oil provided with each machine.

Training offered by such courses as this office procedures class helped prepare students for the growing number of jobs in business.

Efficiency." To the left of the emblem were these words:

> Instigated by the President
> Ordered by the Membership
> Edited (reluctantly) by the Secretary

To the right of the emblem were these:

> Published Intermittently
> Contributions solicited, not in cash but in brain effusion.

That first issue of *Accredited News* contained a report on the Association's finances for 1920. Expenditures totaled $3,019 for the twelve-month period. The largest expense was for travel ($1,029), and the second largest was for stenographic services ($335). The report also showed that $325 was owed by fourteen schools that were behind in their membership payments.

The newsletter was a great success. It was published and distributed several times each year until it was replaced by the *Business School Executive* in 1950.

THE GREAT CHAUTAUQUA CONFERENCE

A grandiose plan was formulated by the Board of Governors to hold a conference for the Association's members in the summer of 1923. This was the first attempt to host a major national meeting of the group apart from the annual gathering in late December. To entice members to attend, the organizers chose to hold the summer event at the Chautauqua meeting grounds in New York State. This was a renowned meeting camp of almost spiritual proportions at the time.

The program began at 9 A.M. on July 16, 1923, in the Pier Building. NAACS president Ben Williams opened the session with forty-six members present. Some had come from as far away as Canada and California. They joined in the singing of patriotic and spiritual songs. The attendees also announced their affiliations with other organizations, such as the Rotarians, Kiwanis, and Lions clubs. One member even stood up and announced that no one had yet declared allegiance to any church affiliation and that he was proud to be a Methodist.

Woodbridge N. Ferris, United States Senator-elect from Michigan, was a key speaker. He gave three separate addresses at Chautauqua on the value of a business education, the importance of education for all, and master teachers. John E. Gill, a member of the Association, was also a featured lecturer. Gill later became known as "the Teddy Roosevelt of Business Education" for his talents as a thinker and orator at the Great Chautauqua Conference.

The Chautauqua event has historic significance because it reflects the issues and thinking that dominated the early days of the Association. In his speeches, Senator-elect Ferris noted "how handicapped the present generation is in trying to keep pace with the evolution of events; the automobile, movie pictures, and the multiplicity of entertainment features, all seeking to undermine stability and continuity of purpose." (Imagine how the good Senator-elect might feel today!)

In addition to focusing on educational concerns, the conference spent time discussing school management. "Effective Methods of Popularizing the Private Business School" was one topic of discussion, and three different speakers presented their points of view. Sessions were held on effective and ethical advertising. Transfer of course credit was also discussed, and a uniform policy acknowledging transfer of credit was promoted. In addition, the transfer of tuition fees was strongly debated at Chautauqua.

Speakers encouraged the members to consider buying their own facilities instead of continuing to lease them: if a school building was purchased intelligently, it would remain a good real estate investment over the years. The conferees noted, as a matter of interest, that in the transition from renting property to buying their own buildings, many schools shortened their names and attached "College" to their title. In Omaha there was Boyles College; in Davenport, Brown's College; in Racine, Moore's College; in Waterloo, Gates College; and in Trenton, Rider College. The question of

THESE MEN ARE LEAVING THE OFFICES—

Who Will Take Their Places?

Largely young women and girls anxious to do so.

But they must be trained, and trained quickly and efficiently. Young women are adept in learning business, and when properly qualified by a Business Training, can transact the affairs of business with the same accuracy and dispatch as the men.

Reprinted from The Proof, *newsletter of Duff's-Iron City Business Institute, September 1917.*

whether the addition of "College" added prestige and dignity to a school was discussed but remained unanswered. Only the passage of time would answer that one.

GOVERNMENT RELATIONS

From its earliest days, the NAACS was concerned with establishing a good relationship with the federal government. In 1916, for example, members of the NAACS began meeting with Dr. Glen Levin Swiggert, specialist in Commercial Education for the United States Bureau of Education, in order to establish an understanding about the roles of private and public school education, and to emphasize that quality educational service was the main concern of the Association. As a result of one such meeting, held at Columbia University, a study was undertaken to assess the need for bookkeeping and other commercial courses, to establish the curriculum requirements of these courses, and to find a way of tailoring these courses to the rapidly developing commercial interests of the times.

Relations with the federal government became stronger during World

"SAFETY FIRST" for Women

Every now and then some widow comes into our school to learn bookkeeping or stenography. The death of her husband has left her dependent upon her own labor.

We believe in "Safety First!" First, before she is married, have your daughter take a thorough commercial course; then she is safe no matter what happens!

—From *The Miami Commercial Bee*

War I. The Board of Governors of the NAACS offered the United States Civil Service Commission the facilities of member schools throughout the country for administering civil service examinations. They also offered to provide a paid expert to the United States Civil Service Examining Board during the war years. As a result, representatives of the NAACS were asked to participate in conferences at the Civil Service headquarters in Washington, D.C., where the difficult problems arising from the abnormal demands of wartime were discussed.

After World War I ended, thousands of disabled soldiers returned from the conflict, unfit for the type of employment to which they had been accustomed. The United States government decided to give these veterans the opportunity to return to the workforce by facilitating retraining within the range of their physical limitations. Many of these veterans chose to be trained for office work or other business-related activity.

The government had wanted to establish special training schools throughout the country. The Association, viewed as a friend in the war effort by the federal government, asked to be part of the rehabilitation program. Since the Association already had strong programs of study and facilities in all parts of the country, the federal government was quick to agree. Although actual figures are unavailable, it is known that many World War I veterans received their training in NAACS schools as part of this joint rehabilitation effort.

During the 1920s the relationship between the Association and the federal and state governments grew. Officials and legislators from both federal and state governments were invited to Association conventions and regional meetings. In addition, state education officials and members of the United

States Bureau of Education served on NAACS curriculum committees. These committees designed model courses of study that were eventually offered at many NAACS schools throughout the country.

The 1920s were prosperous for almost everyone, including private career schools, but the Great Depression brought economic growth to an abrupt halt, and then into a spiraling decline. Many business schools survived surprisingly well during the Depression years. Still, these were not years of fond memories for private-sector educators. Many people could not afford tuition. Furthermore, there was great concern among the membership of the Association when the Federal Emergency Relief Act was passed in 1933. In Chicago alone, thirty-one new "free schools" were reported to have opened shortly after the Relief Act passed. Under the terms of this New Deal legislation, commercial schools had to offer commercial subjects "free of charge" to those who needed them.

The members of NAACS did not oppose free commercial education for those who could not afford to pay, but they did want the terms of qualification to be clearly defined. The Roosevelt administration established a committee that included officers of the NAACS and Harry Hopkins, Director of the Federal Emergency Relief Administration. After lengthy discussions, a decision was reached about who could enroll. On July 2, 1935, Dr. Hopkins specified that "beginning classes in standard commercial subjects may not enroll anyone except unemployed adults who are on relief."

Thus, for the time being, a major threat from the public sector was held off. Little did the membership realize how much the public sector would eventually contribute to vocational education in the decades to come.

On December 28, 1936, at its annual meeting in Cleveland, the Association adopted a resolution petitioning the federal government to allow students applying for government assistance to select the educational institution of their choice. In addition, the Association requested that the federal government grant "duly inspected" private career schools the same privileges that public institutions had under the public-assistance program. Apparently, the issue was never resolved to the satisfaction of Association members, and the new competition from the public sector added to the Association's woes. Commercial education by the public sector, which arose in response to the hard times of the Depression, remains a dominant force in American education today.

ACCREDITATION ACTIVITIES

As noted earlier, "accredited" in the title of the Association referred to a school's acceptance for membership and its adherence to a code of ethics and management policy prescribed by the organization. During its first twenty-five years, the Association conducted no accrediting activities as specific or extensive as those practiced today. However, even in the early days, the leaders of NAACS clearly understood the need to develop a system of self-evaluation and inspection for the benefit of all members.

The Vigilance Committee (renamed the Better Business Bureau in 1923) was charged with monitoring the activities of the membership to determine compliance with the Association's stated ethical and managerial policies. As time passed, the committee began to send representatives to new schools applying for membership in order to determine that the schools had the necessary teachers, staff, equipment, and facilities to meet the requirements of an accredited member. This activity continued to develop informally until the time of the Great Depression.

Since the earliest days of the Association's founding, many members wanted the accreditation aspect of membership to become more formal-

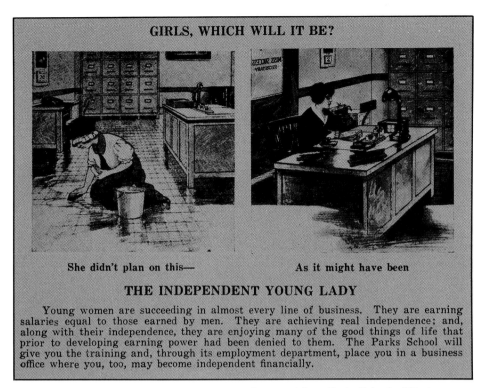

Reprinted from Parks School of Business catalog.

Draughon's Business College in the early 1930s.

Typing class at Miami-Jacobs College in the 1930s.

By 1927 the Association realized that it would need to review and upgrade its own standards for membership in order to provide quality career education in a growing business climate. State Supervisor of Trade and Industrial Education for the Commonwealth of Virginia, B. H. Van Opt, suggested to the Association that the easiest way to set up standards was to follow the practices of the "usual accrediting agencies." Areas to be evaluated included qualifications for teachers, minimum entrance requirements for students, minimum course lengths, minimum equipment requirements, model courses of study, and graduation requirements.

Based on Van Opt's suggestions, a series of "Standards of Practice" was formulated by the Association in the mid-1920s. The historical record indicates that standards of practice absorbed a great deal of discussion time among the members at conventions and regional meetings in the latter part of the 1920s. Standards were numbered and titled, and members were asked to write position papers to clarify each standard and give examples of schools that were in or out of compliance with them.

In addition to the adoption of standards of practice, a "system of inspection" was voted into existence by the membership. Since there were about three hundred member schools in 1927, the inspection process focused on new applications for membership and on member schools that found themselves in financial, managerial, or educational hardship.

Members in good standing were usually asked to serve on inspection teams. Because of the burdens of travel, inspection teams were usually composed of members in the same geographical area as the school to be visited. The application prepared by the school to be inspected was quite rudimentary compared with the present self-study document required by the Accrediting Commission of the AICS.

Clearly, accreditation had become a very important, although still informal, activity of the Association as it approached its twenty-fifth birthday. Even as far back as the first years of the NAACS, members were re-

ized. It was finally decided that NAACS should try to develop a relationship with the North Central Association of Colleges and Secondary Schools in the hope of obtaining their services as an accrediting agency for the commercial-school membership of NAACS. The North Central Association was a pioneer in regional accreditation and had a strong national reputation.

The attempt to form an alliance with North Central grew hot and then cold over a number of years. In 1923, North Central passed a resolution stating "that this Association accept the principle of admitting to the approved list of the Association, as secondary schools Private Commercial Colleges, and that it instruct the Commission on secondary schools to proceed with the accreditation of such institutions on the basis of existing standards and to report to the Association later any revision of these standards that it wishes to recommend."

Records show that the North Central Association accredited some of the NAACS member schools from time to time. But in the long run, the alliance never really took hold, and the relationship eventually diminished and disappeared. The literature does not explain why the relationship never developed, but it is clear that many attempts at an alliance did take place.

quired to state carefully the term "fully accredited" and to display the emblem of the NAACS. The issue of accreditation, however, was not as intense in the 1930s, when, because of the Great Depression, few new schools entered the Association and many of the older members ceased operations.

THE SILVER ANNIVERSARY

Ordinarily, a fledgling organization does not make as big an occasion out of its twenty-fifth birthday as NAACS did in 1937. Perhaps NAACS did so because many of its founders and original leaders still served in key positions, such as the president and secretary, both of whom had served since 1912. Although the reason for their going all-out in celebrating may not be clear, their December 28 anniversary banquet certainly turned out to be a memorable event.

The Hotel Sherman in Chicago was chosen as the site of the twenty-fifth anniversary celebration. This seemed appropriate, since the same hotel had served as the site for many previous conventions, and Chicago was the birthplace of the Association. President Ben Williams greeted the celebrants, and the "Silver Anniversary Annual Banquet" began at 6:30 P.M. on December 28, 1937. It was Williams's twenty-fifth year as leader of the Association, and he had announced the year before that he would retire as president after the anniversary celebration.

As tradition dictated, a prominent educator or government official was invited to address the gathering. The key speaker was Dr. D. W. Daniel, head of the Department of General Science of Clemson College in Clemson, South Carolina. Daniel was not originally scheduled to speak. Filling in at the last minute, he made his address brief, and those present expressed their appreciation with a standing round of applause. It should be noted that Dr. Aubrey Williams, Executive Director of the National Youth Administration, was the scheduled speaker, but for unknown reasons he did not attend the banquet.

Former Governor Eberhart of Min-

Reprinted from Accredited News.

nesota was also invited to give a presentation. He, too, had not been on the program originally. However, by coincidence, he met Ben Williams in the hotel lobby earlier that day. Williams, delighted to see his longtime friend, asked Eberhart to participate in the festivities.

After the speeches, Williams presented certificates to all of the charter-member schools who were still with the organization. At least a dozen of them were still in the fold and were so honored.

Hubert Porter, Secretary of the Association, took the podium to recognize Ben Williams's contribution of twenty-five years of distinguished service. A citation was presented to Williams with the designation "The Honorary Degree of Doctor of Laws." The degree contained the official seal of the organization and the signatures of the members of the Board. The honor was well deserved and technically within the purview of the Association. The charter of 1917 did, in fact, authorize the NAACS to grant honorary degrees.

At this point in the program, Dr. Benjamin Franklin Williams left the presidency of NAACS. It had been twenty-five years of hard work, through good and bad times, but he viewed the results as well worth the effort. His successor, Dr. Edward M. Hull, had served the organization as Vice President of the Eastern Division, and as Chairman of the Education Committee. Dr. Hull was from Banks College in Philadelphia, and his candidacy had received unanimous support.

POTPOURRI

A large number of isolated issues, people stories, and humorous happenings weaved their way through the early history of the Association. Space does not permit a visit to all of them, but several of the more interesting ones are touched on in the following paragraphs:

- The Association was constantly concerned about competitive associations. They denied accusations that they prohibited more than one accredited member to operate in any one town or city. They stated that no such rule, written or otherwise, existed, yet these accusations served as a good excuse for other "accrediting" organizations to spring up. NAACS leaders felt, and openly proclaimed, that associations trying to copy them provided a path for those who were not up to the high standards of the Association.

- When radio joined the newspaper industry as a popular means of communication in the 1930s, member schools soon began to sponsor local programs. Various members of the Association suggested to the Board that the organization do some advertising about the benefits of private career schools in general, and the advantages to students attending NAACS member institutions. Some radio spots were purchased by the Association, and at one point it seriously considered sponsoring a regularly scheduled show. But the timing was not right, and the Depression halted all efforts in this regard.

- Another project that never got off the ground was the establishment of a national university owned and operated by NAACS. When the Association was incorporated in Washington, D.C., in 1917, one of the powers granted to it was the right to award degrees under the authority of a national university. The authorization included, "professorships in mathematics, accounting, law, banking, etc., and to ordain and grant suitable certificates, diplomas, and degrees." In 1932 a proposal to activate the university was made, and a plan of action was presented. However, like other costly projects during the Depression years, this one soon faded away.

- People were always in the forefront of Association activities. In May 1932, *Accredited News* presented an article and portrait honoring John Robert Gregg. Gregg was cited for having just received an honorary lifetime membership in the National Commercial Teachers Federation at the Federation's annual meeting in Chicago. Many NAACS members belonged to the Federation, and a close bond had always existed between the two organizations. The article explained that "this recognition puts us in a reminiscent mood, many of us who also have been members of the Federation . . . we think of the achievements of John R. Gregg . . . what they have meant to us as individuals and what they have meant to hundreds of thousands."

- *Accredited News* proudly noted in the November 1936 issue that seven members of the B. L. Cristy family were alumni of the same member school. The four young men and three young ladies all attended Brown's Business College in Galesburg, Illinois. The article, with photographs of all seven of them, stated: "There are ten members in the family and seven have, or will, graduate; Shirley J. is now in school; Wayne M. is in the coal business; Lyall is employed as chief clerk in the General Superintendents Office, C. B. & Q. R. R.; Ruth is in civil service in Washington, D.C.; Andrew J. and Lynn C. are employed in the City; and Gertrude F. was with Doyle Furniture prior to her marriage."

Opportunities for women were always an important concern of Association members. As early as 1926, Hiram N. Rasely of Burdett College in Boston delivered a radio message on station WEEL in Boston on "Business and Its Opportunities for Women." Rasely said, "Most satisfactory progress, in the world of business, comes to those women who possess a good basic education; . . . who have mastered the art of writing shorthand; . . . operate the typewriter with facility; . . . can use the English language correctly and effectively; who are well versed in the science of accounts; who have learned fundamental principles of economics, business organization and management; and who have an appreciation for good literature."

Office procedures class at Utica School of Commerce in the mid-1930s.

The contribution of women to educational services was highlighted in *Accredited News* in July 1930. That issue contained a lengthy article entitled "Brief Sketches of Women Executives." It contained biographies of seventeen women who were active in the management of private career schools, from Seattle, Washington, to Paterson, New Jersey.

THE PARADOX

The Association not only survived, but thrived, during its first twenty-five years. Paradoxically, stability and change, in combination, were the keys to its success.

Stability was reflected in the outstanding leadership of the key players who founded the alliance and served as its officers for many years. Strong leadership enabled the Association to deal with change. The NAACS was flexible and responsive to the rapidly evolving socioeconomic environment and the shifting trends in private career education. Throughout this time, the NAACS, by its efforts, remained true to its mission: to promote and maintain quality educational programs and sound business practices.

Ernest H. Brooks II, now president of the
Brooks Institute, follows in the footsteps of
his father, Ernest H. Brooks, the Institute's founder.

Chapter 4

On to the Gold (1937–1962)

The year is 1937. President Franklin D. Roosevelt signs the United States Neutrality Act as dark clouds of war gather over the world. Meanwhile, in Berlin, Benito Mussolini confers with Adolf Hitler. England has a new monarch, George VI, and Neville Chamberlain becomes prime minister. Back home, the Lincoln Tunnel opens, providing a new link between New Jersey and New York City. And on the West Coast, the Golden Gate Bridge, arching across San Francisco Bay, officially opens for business.

Snow White and the Seven Dwarfs hits movie screens across the country in glorious technicolor, and the Steinbeck classic *Of Mice and Men* fills book shelves. *Babes in Arms*, a musical comedy by Rodgers and Hart, captivates Broadway audiences. The hit tunes in the dance halls are "The Lady Is a Tramp," "Whistle While You Work," "A Foggy Day in London Town," "Harbor Lights," and "I've Got My Love To Keep Me Warm."

In sports, the United States tennis team wins the Davis Cup from England, while Pittsburgh shuts out Washington 21–0 in the Rose Bowl. In a subway showdown, the New York Yankees take the World Series 4–1 over the Giants. And all ears are glued to the radio, as Joe Louis wins the heavyweight crown back from Jim Braddock.

The sad news of 1937 included the explosion of the German airship *Hindenburg* over Lakehurst, New Jersey, the untimely death of George Gershwin, and the disappearance of Amelia Earhart somewhere in the Pacific Ocean. It was in this historic environment that the Association celebrated its twenty-fifth birthday and moved into its twenty-sixth year.

HISTORICAL OVERVIEW

The period from 1937 to 1962 was the most traumatic in the modern history of this nation. World War II touched the lives of all Americans. Although our land and its people were never assaulted at home the way

Original home of Robinson Business College and its founders.

Europeans were, the human and material sacrifices made by this country are still remembered by many. We survived the war and picked up our lives and moved on in new and exciting directions.

The postwar recovery years brought some welcome changes. People could buy refrigerators and finally discard leaky ice boxes. New cars became available, replacing worn-out, old jalopies. Sugar, gasoline, nylons, and beef were becoming plentiful again. Factories stopped manufacturing war products and, instead, concentrated energy and manpower on fulfilling the seemingly insatiable demands for new consumer goods. The economic and social woes of the Great Depression were in the past, and planned housing developments popped up like crocuses across suburban landscapes. Drive-in theaters and shopping malls rapidly followed the move away from urban centers.

The optimism and economic prosperity that began after World War II continued as the Association progressed toward its fiftieth birthday. Of course, these years were not without setbacks. The Korean War renewed fears of rationing and sacrifice, and the Cold War was like a dark cloud over our heads. Still, the nation was

relatively stable and Americans took advantage of educational opportunities and moved up the socioeconomic ladder. Through the G.I. Bill and guaranteed government loans, many veterans were able to further their education, buy homes, and start businesses. As the demand for quality education increased, the private career sector played a larger role in providing educational options.

History shows that one by-product of war is the proliferation of new technologies. This was especially so after World War II. The rise of atomic energy is one example of this increase in technology. Other examples include the development of the U.S. space program and the sweeping advances in civilian aviation after the war. New discoveries in medical applications and pharmacology were the direct result of medical care on the battlefield. The development of the transistor led to fantastic advances in electronics. New types of automated equipment eased workloads and filled leisure hours.

In education, advances were also being made at a rapid rate. As the job market opened up, so did the demand for new programs of study, modern equipment, and facilities.

Educational associations also proliferated after World War II. In 1942 the first chapter of the Future Business Leaders of America (FBLA) was formed in Johnson City, Tennessee. This was certainly an appropriate organization for the times. In July 1946 the National Education Association Department of Business Education and the National Council for Business Education merged to form the United Business Education Association (UBEA). In 1950 the Southern Business Education Association was formed as a regional unit of the UBEA, and in 1952 the Mountain-Plains Business Education Association, another regional unit, was founded. In 1962, the UBEA was renamed the National Business Education Association, and the Eastern Business Education Association was established as a regional unit of the organization.

In 1953 the long-awaited National Center for Higher Education in Washington, D.C., was erected. Also in that year, the prestigious John Robert Gregg Award was granted for the first time. The award, jointly sponsored by the McGraw-Hill Book Company and the UBEA, is given to outstanding business educators. The first recipient of the award was Professor Frederick G. Nichols, a friend and long-time associate in private career education.

PREWAR ISSUES

Even before World War II some significant issues had begun to bubble on the burners of the Association and its member schools. Some were influenced by the threat of war, others not.

One major issue confronting the Association concerned the policies for awarding scholarships. Member schools had previously granted scholarships based on a student's potential for academic achievement or on financial need. However, a few schools used these scholarships to fill vacant seats in classrooms by offering reduced tuition. In such cases, neither ability nor need were considered.

Association President Edward Hull referred to these practices in his annual message to the members in December 1939. He said: "It is not the use of scholarships that is objectionable. It is their misuse—the abuse of them. A scholarship honestly given, that is, given in the right way, to the right person, and for the right purpose is ethical. . . . On the other hand, any member of the National Association of Accredited Commercial Schools who misuses the scholarship feature should be dropped from membership."

During this same year, Jay Miller, of Goldey Beacom College in Wilmington, Delaware, proposed that the Association establish an "idea exchange." Recognizing the mutual benefits of sharing information and experience, Miller suggested that the Association set up a bureau where members could exchange ideas for educational programs and management techniques on a continual basis. Before Miller's proposal could be put into effect, World War II intervened.

Another issue of vital importance to the survival and growth of private

Bookkeeping class at Ohio Valley Business College, circa 1942.

Tampa Business College.

1939 World's Fair in New York City.

The Golden Gate Bridge changed the economic and social life of the San Francisco Bay area and became a symbol of the West as well.

Who could forget this tender scene from Gone With the Wind *starring Clark Gable and Vivian Leigh?*

WPA FEDERAL THEATRE PRESENTS

IT CAN'T HAPPEN HERE

DRAMATIZED BY
Sinclair Lewis & J.C.Moffitt

ADELPHI THEATRE
54th Street East of 7th Ave.

Poster from the theater project of the Works Progress Administration.

Charlie Chaplin ridiculed Hitler's dream of world conquest in the 1940 movie The Great Dictator. *Although the film produced mostly mixed reactions, it was a smash hit in wartime Britain.*

FDR in classic pose with the cigarette
holder that became his trademark.

Bill Mauldin, the unofficial spokesman for
the enlisted man, sketches his view of
World War II.

Willie and Joe, the battle-weary twosome,
were featured in Mauldin's most famous
cartoons.

The magic of the moment! Times Square
in New York City on V-J Day.

An atomic bomb raises a great mushroom
cloud over Nagasaki, Japan.

Raising the flag on Iwo Jima. This Pulitzer
Prize-winning photograph served as a model
for many war memorials.

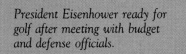

President Eisenhower ready for golf after meeting with budget and defense officials.

A lone soldier standing guard as nine black students enter the all-white Little Rock Central High School in Arkansas.

Special Army Counsel Joseph Welch (left) and Senator Joseph McCarthy talk after reaching an agreement on monitored phone calls between Pentagon officials and senators.

Hula hoop-mania across America.

Jackie Robinson steals home against the
Chicago Cubs in 1952.

Elvis Presley appears on the "Ed Sullivan
Show" in 1956.

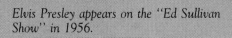

Reprinted from The National News, *September 1938.*

career schools was the increased competition from the public-school sector. The Board of the Association encouraged members to coordinate their educational concerns with public-school educators through participation in other recognized educational organizations.

Furthermore, in order to remain competitive with public schools, private career schools updated their curricula and expanded their schedules to include night classes. One especially innovative example was that of Pace Institute in New York City. Pace administrators recognized the need to provide quality programs at convenient times by offering special summer day and evening sessions. They increased the number of evening and Saturday classes during the regular school year as well. Intensive courses at convenient times became a Pace specialty, and the idea worked. The response was tremendous, and Pace Institute continued to grow despite keen competition from the public sector of commercial education in New York City.

In 1941 an interesting question was put before the Association: Should NAACS schools offer a program of study in the Cherokee Indian language? Leonard E. Crawford, President of American College in Tulsa, Oklahoma, had instituted such a program at his school. The program was successful at American College, and a suggestion was made to offer similar programs at other schools in the area. Once again, however, the war intervened and priorities changed.

DELTA NU OMEGA—THETA ALPHA CHI

A plan for a system of fraternities and sororities under the sponsorship of the Association had been on the drawing board for a number of years. It was at the annual meeting of 1938 that the plan was reintroduced and met with enthusiasm from the members. Charles Walker of Portland, Oregon, spoke for the proposal, and the plan was finally approved for implementation at the 1940 annual convention.

At an interim meeting of the Association's Board of Governors, in July 1940, the program of fraternities and sororities was finalized. It called for twenty chapters to be installed by the end of September 1940, and fifty by the end of June 1941. By August 1940, ten sororities and five fraternities had been granted charters by NAACS, and applications for ten other chapters were being processed. The Board appointed Hiram N. Rasely, of Burdett College in Boston, as Grand President of the fraternity/sorority program. The fraternities were named Delta Nu Omega, and the sororities Theta Alpha Chi.

Although each chapter had the authority to develop its own program, the Board established a common activity program to serve as a guideline for individual groups. The program included monthly meeting procedures, educational activities, a social-events calendar, and an annual chapter banquet agenda. Philanthropic and community-service activities were emphasized as the key function of the organizations. Chapters were expected to lend assistance to community projects, such as helping the poor at Christmas, conducting food sales for the homeless and hungry, and raising funds for charities and educational scholarships. As part of the common program, a national newsletter was planned for distribution to the chapters.

Each fraternity and sorority chapter chose its own leaders. This provided students with the opportunity to develop poise as well as experience in representing their peers. Participating in chapter activities provided many students with a way to achieve their personal goals.

Rituals, such as pledge procedures, were the "binding force" in the fraternity and sorority movement. Initiation materials and the pledge-ceremony procedures for each chapter to follow were carefully detailed. A portion of chapter dues was sent to the Grand President to pay for the costs of coordinating programs and providing materials for ceremonies.

By February 1941, there were thirty-seven chapters in schools across the country. Several chapters had sent representatives to the annual NAACS convention in Chicago the previous December. Many of the new chapters had exciting plans for future social and community activities. It was a spirited movement. Unfortunately, the entry of the United States into World War II required a dedication to more serious endeavors.

STIFF BUT FRIENDLY RIVALRY

Some dissension had begun to grow within the NAACS in the 1930s and the organization had to struggle to maintain membership numbers and interest. The country was emerging from the hard times of the Depression, and the threat of war didn't make things any better. Many career educators, both public and private, struggled during these years, and, once again, education took a back seat as the United States became involved in the war.

In 1931 a stiff but friendly competition began with the establishment of another business-school organization. The Southern Accredited Business Colleges merged with the American Association of Vocational Schools to form the American Association of Business Schools (AABS), a formidable alliance whose membership was vibrant and aggressive. The new organization appointed C. W. Woodward, of Burlington Business College in Burlington, Iowa, as its executive secretary. It also began publishing a newsletter called *The Compass*. This was the forerunner of *AICS Compass* that is presently published, and we will see how that story unfolded as our history progresses.

Eventually, this AABS changed its name to the American Association of Commercial Colleges (AACC), but the form and structure of the association remained unchanged. Like NAACS, it held its conventions during the last week of the year, and its mission was also to establish high standards of academics for its members and for the private career sector as a whole.

The American Association of Commercial Colleges grew in strength and numbers as 1940 approached. Periodically *The Compass* published impressive lists of new member schools. The AACC did not stress accreditation as an activity and, in fact, questioned the authority of any organization to say that it was the accreditor

Students at Katharine Gibbs School practice typing skills.

Military graduation, Tampa Business College, 1941.

of member schools. AACC was an outstanding vehicle for communication and fellowship for its members for over thirty years, until an event in the early sixties ended its independence.

WAR EMERGENCY COUNCIL

On reflection, it seems bizarre that World War II hit like a tornado since most of the news releases at the time indicated a country preparing for war. The nation's entry into the war brought Americans together with a singleness of purpose. They were dedicated to meeting the challenges of war and to securing freedom for the Allies.

Many Americans gave their lives and limbs. The people back home sacrificed their loved ones, their careers, and their comforts. Education and training for careers slowed to a crawl while training for the war effort, coordinated by the United States Departments of War and of the Navy, accelerated. Almost half of the student population of private career schools went off to war. Many of the students who remained, primarily women, left school to join in the civil defense effort.

The leaders in the private career schools wanted to help in the war effort as much as possible, as well as

ensure that their schools survived. However, with two major professional organizations, NAACS and AACC, the private sector was fragmented and confused. Dr. J. S. Noffsinger, Director of the National Home Study Council in Washington, D.C., and a spokesman for education, was asked to help.

Dr. Noffsinger called for a War Emergency Council of private business schools, and invited representatives from NAACS, AACC, and nonaffiliated schools to a meeting in Chicago. The meeting, held on December 30, 1942, was convenient for both organizations since both were in Chicago at the time for their annual meetings.

The primary purpose of the council was to make federal and state officials aware of the private business-school facilities that could be utilized during periods of national emergency. In effect, the council served as the voice in Washington for all private career business schools on matters related to the war effort. The council's concerns extended beyond utilizing private career facilities to include programs of study, educational policies, and personnel directed at the war effort.

The War Emergency Council was governed by a board of fifteen members, which later became known as the Council of Fifteen. Five board members were elected by the members of the National Association of Accredited Commercial Schools, five by the members of the American Association of Commercial Colleges, and five representatives came from nonaffiliated private business schools.

President Edward Hull and former President Ben Williams were elected to represent NAACS on the Board. C. W. Woodward of AACC was elected as one of the representatives for his organization. S. L. Fisher, President of Fisher College in Boston, and G. A. Spaulding, President of the Bryant and Stratton Business Institute in Buffalo, were among the nonaffiliates elected to the Board.

The first order of business of the council was to choose its officers. The council elected Hiram N. Rasely, of Burdett College in Boston, president; E. G. Purvis, of Strayer College in

MIGHTY OAKS FROM LITTLE
ACORNS GROW

DADDY OF THEM ALL

| Private Business Schools | Commercial High Schools | Private Business Schools Daddy of them All | Business Departments of Universities | Commercial High Schools | Private Business Schools -- Daddy of them All | Business Departments of Universities |

Reprinted from The Compass.

Washington, D.C., vice president; and C. W. Woodward, secretary.

At the time of the first meeting of the council there were approximately 1,800 private business schools located in all forty-eight states and the District of Columbia. Enrollment in these schools was about 125,000, although the estimated capacity in the schools was about twice that. Obviously, the private sector was ready and eager to serve.

This alliance fostered many new insights into private career education. Among these was a heightened awareness and a broader understanding of the influence of the private career sector. Previously private career educators had traveled to Washington infrequently. With the formation of the War Emergency Council, however, Washington became the center of activity and representation for the private career sector.

The council had some formidable issues to address. One of the most important of these was convincing the federal government to include the private career schools in clerical training programs for the War and Navy Departments. Another was the acquisition of typewriters. The war had created an unusually high demand for typewriters, both here and abroad. At the same time that the demand was growing, supplies were dwindling as manufacturing companies ceased production to concentrate on defense manufacturing priorities. For schools that were training workers for defense purposes, the need for such equipment was even more pronounced, and the council was their only hope. The scarcity of typewriters during the war

Typing from dictation at Ohio Valley Business School.

One of the first commercially successful electric typewriters, circa 1940.

was a particular hardship for business schools. Next to teachers, typewriters were their most important instructional resource. The schools had been called upon to donate typewriters to the war effort. Association member schools gave up many machines to the government for military use.

On October 22, 1945, Harry B. Mitchell, President of the United States Civil Service Commission, wrote George A. Meadows, of Meadows-Draughon College in Shreveport, Louisiana, editor of *Accredited News*, a letter of commendation to the membership. Mitchell stated, ". . . sincere appreciation of the great service rendered by the more than two hundred members of the National Association of Accredited Commercial Schools of this country in the training of thousands of persons in business courses which fitted them especially for duty with the war establishments of the Government as well as with private industry." The Association was very proud of this recognition of the sacrifices made by member schools to help further, in every way they could, the cause of free society.

The private schools also wanted to be contract trainers for the supplementary clerical workers program of the United States Office of Education. The education office had received an appropriation for the training of clerical personnel to meet the needs on the home front during the war. However, the contracts were with public schools and colleges. Naturally, the private sector wanted some of the business, and it was hoped that the War Emergency Council could facilitate an arrangement.

Although the NAACS did wholeheartedly support and participate in the war efforts of the council, the Association had its own agenda. NAACS leaders knew that the war would end eventually, and they wanted the organization to be as vital a force in private career education in the future as it had been in the past. In *Accredited News* in August 1943, the new president of NAACS, Dr. P. S. Spangler, stated: "The work of the Council and that of the Association are not in conflict at any point; in fact, they dovetail into each other and are complementary and supplementary rather than antagonistic. With the return of several million young soldiers and sailors to their home communities, the problem of further education for useful civilian lives will become acute. It will be a problem that can and should be solved from the educational side and belongs therefore to the schools individually and collectively. In this postwar problem the National Association can serve effectively—and will do so."

By early 1945, it was clear the war would soon end. It was also clear the War Emergency Council could not continue under its original mandate or title. Therefore, in 1945, the organization was restructured and renamed the National Council of Business Schools. Rasely stayed on as president, and the new association became a close friend and competitor of NAACS in the postwar era.

POSTWAR OPPORTUNITIES

As the production problems of the war years ceased, distribution problems began. In December 1945 *The Busi-*

ness School Executive, the official publication of the National Council of Business Schools, observed: "An unprecedented number of the highest caliber young people should be attracted to the field of distribution. The private business school has a unique opportunity to render a national service by stressing the needs and the opportunities within this field to those who should be interested, and to supplement their basic training in stenography, secretaryship, and accounting with courses in the broad field of distribution—advertising, sales, promotion, merchandising and personal selling."

Accredited News, in May 1947, also recognized the opportunities in distribution for private career schools when it stated: "One of the most promising occupational fields open to young people from now on will be in the field of retail selling. Like any other business or profession, proper methods of contacting the public can now be taught, with many attractive openings for both sexes in the Nation's great stores."

The article went on to cite a series of films by Jam Handy entitled "Behind the Counter," which were being used for instructional purposes at such leading stores as R. H. Macy & Company, Lord & Taylor, A. I. Namm, and Kresge. The article also stressed that visual aids would be an important aspect of the instructional program for teaching retailing.

AN OBLIGING CLERK

The clerk was most obliging, but the young woman customer was hard to please. Roll after roll of blankets did he patiently take down and show her; nothing suited.

For some fifteen minutes this mock sale went on, then the young woman said condescendingly. "Well, I don't intend to buy. I was just looking for a friend."

"Wait a moment please," cried the clerk. "There is one more blanket left on the shelf. Maybe you will find your friend in it."

— From Accredited News

Court reporting became another growing field after the war. There was a great demand for qualified court reporters, and their availability was limited. Schools were encouraged to establish programs of study in court reporting, and to assist in the development of professional standards in the field. Many existing schools added court reporting to their programs, and many new schools opened their doors with courses in court reporting.

Other new and expanded programs were offered by private career schools in 1946. The Dale Carnegie Public Speaking Courses were among the most popular of these. The Elmer Wheeler Salesmanship course, as well as courses in charm or personality development, also attracted scores of interested students. Similarly, there was an increased demand for secretarial courses in the medical and legal fields.

Business-school students in the postwar era seemed more serious about their academic studies than students before the war had been. Many of these new students were veterans or older adults seeking reintegration into a consumer-oriented, white-collar work force. New standards for courses, teachers, and school facilities were implemented to meet the demands of the new breed of students. Night schools became popular, and many schools were forced to offer more than one session to meet the increased demand.

The postwar times were good for the Association. Records show that 96 percent of member schools had higher daytime enrollments in 1946 than in 1945, and 80 percent reported greater evening enrollments as well. Most of the schools had more male students than female, mostly because of the number of veterans enrolled. Almost 40 percent of the schools reported that they were filled to capacity during day classes, and 14 percent stated their evening classes were also at capacity.

Most of the new breed of students in private career schools were veterans. Their war experiences had left them with a broader perspective on a great many issues, and they openly expressed their views in the classroom. They had definite ideas about instruction, and passed their ideas on to teachers and administrators. The schools, in turn, were responsive to their needs, adapting class procedures and trying new approaches to accommodate the veterans.

Private business schools in Ohio provided a special example of cooperation and response to the influx of veterans. Ten of the leading business schools and colleges involved in veteran education conducted a special forum at the meeting of the Ohio Business Schools Association in Columbus, in May 1946. Representatives at this conference shared information and ideas relating to the "problems, pleasures and procedures incident to the training of veterans in private business schools." Similar meetings were held in other locations, too. The private sector was once again doing what it did best, responding quickly to the needs of its students and the society it serves.

Association conventions had been suspended for several years as a result of government restrictions during the war. Leo Blackburn, Chairman of the

Board of Southeastern Business College in Chillicothe, Ohio, recently recalled the first convention after the war: "I am perhaps the only AICS member left who attended those first postwar conventions in Chicago, the first in 1947 at the now razed Edgewater Beach Hotel. I remember that convention rather vividly as it was my first contact with the then leaders of the field. At that 1947 meeting, and the next few, the man who seemed to be most respected and most dearly loved was Hiram Rasely. He and a few others, Jay Miller in particular, had apparently waged a heroic and uphill battle on Capitol Hill to gain G.I. Bill recognition for proprietary schools. At the second or third convention I attended, a gift of $1,000 (solicited from active members) was, as a surprise, presented to Hiram Rasely at the final banquet. This presentation and its acceptance was certainly an unforgettable and deeply moving scene. Hiram Rasely actually broke down and cried, so filled was he with this show of gratitude, love, and respect. It was evident that Hiram Rasely had put our organization far before his own interests and had worked many months as our Washington Watch Dog."

The Serviceman's Readjustment Act of 1944 was one of the most enlightened pieces of legislation ever enacted by Congress. Known as the G.I. Bill of Rights, this legislation's most widely utilized benefits were in the area of education. Under this bill, veterans who had served at least ninety days in the military after September 16, 1940, and were honorably discharged were automatically entitled to one year of full-time training plus a period equal to their time of service. The maximum entitlement was forty-eight months of educational instruction to be funded by the federal government. Public Laws 268 and 411 further refined and increased benefits in subsequent years.

Private career schools were not included as eligible institutions in the first draft of the G.I. Bill, even though private career leaders had worked so diligently at gaining recognition. However, the private-school leaders were persistent, and, after overcoming numerous obstacles, private career

Christmas party at Draughon's Business College in 1948.

schools were formally recognized as eligible institutions. Hiram Rasely gave a great deal of credit to Senator Robert Taft of Ohio for helping advance the cause of the private career sector. Although Taft was a conservative, he believed that the scope of educational benefits for veterans should be as broad as possible.

The 1952 Veteran's Readjustment Assistance Act, the G.I. Bill of Rights for veterans of the Korean War, provided similar educational opportunities for veterans. Again, private career schools were included within the scope of the legislation.

GOVERNMENT INTERACTION

Relations between NAACS and the federal government were at their lowest point during World War II. It was not a matter of inadequate communication or willful neglect of the private sector, but simply the case of a government besieged with problems far greater than the state of private career education.

The Association did establish a "Washington Committee" in order to get legislators to include private career schools in their various funded training programs. "Short courses" were in demand, and the government had contracted with public-education agencies to be the exclusive providers of these courses. Naturally, the private sector felt left out. This was especially true for short courses related to typewriting, shorthand, record keeping, and accounting. In addition to feeling overlooked, private-school educators expressed concerns about how much could really be taught in short courses, and whether quality was being sacrificed to meet learning-productivity quotas.

The Association appointed itself watchdog for maintaining high standards for civil service entrance examinations. During the war there had been an attempt to lower civil service test score qualifications in order to fill certain government jobs. NAACS representatives worked with the United States Department of Education to ensure that standards were main-

Nashville City Champions 1953, Draughon's Business College.

tained. Together these agencies expressed the viewpoint that "we'd rather have one good stenographer in Washington than three poor ones." The Association wanted to shorten courses and prepare people for the civil-service exams by "intensification and not by amputation."

Shortly after taking office in 1952, President Eisenhower proposed a "White House Conference on Education." This was a welcome action since education had been at the bottom of the priorities list during the war and the early recovery years. Public Law 530 (82nd Congress, Second Session) stipulated that the White House conference be held prior to November 30, 1955, and that it be "broadly representative of educators and other interested citizens from all parts of the nation." Further, it would "consider and report to the President on significant and pressing problems in the field of education."

Members of the Association welcomed the conference as an opportunity to make their voices heard. However, the emphasis of the conference was on the problems of elementary and secondary public schools and on their general need for more teachers. In his closing remarks, Neil McElroy, Chairman of the White House conference, and President of the Procter and Gamble Company, emphasized that Americans believe in competition, but only in fair competition. This is why education must provide opportunities for all people

Advertising layout for International Business College.

Doorway to success, Miami-Jacobs College.

gaged to count the ballots. On June 2, 1949, at 5 P.M., with all the votes received and counted, the CPAs announced the results:

	Yes	No
NAACS	316	83
NCBS	86	36
AACC	28	92
Total	430	211

Although members of NAACS and NCBS were overwhelmingly in favor of the proposal, AACC rejected it by a three to one vote. It was a blow to the plan, but the effort still went forward. It had been agreed before the election that if only one of the three associations turned down the consolidation proposal, the other two would still consolidate.

In August 1949 the boards of NAACS and the National Council met to work out the details of consolidation. The suggested name of the Association was the National Association and Council of Business Schools. An interim committee would govern the NACBS in the beginning.

The annual conventions of NAACS, NCBS, and, surprisingly, the AACC, were held jointly in November 1949, at the Edgewater Beach Hotel in Chicago. At the meeting the members of NAACS and NCBS were asked to approve the first details of consolidation. It was an emotional event. Many of the old-timers who had founded NAACS, including Ben Williams, were present. There was much debate, but eventually everyone voted their conscience, and the approval was finalized.

President George Meadows of NAACS and Hiram Rasely of NCBS gave brief messages and their blessings to consolidation at the November convention. This was followed by a joint meeting of the two boards of governors. The first order of business was the election of interim officers of the governing committee of the consolidated Association. It was agreed that E. R. Maetzold of Minneapolis, Minnesota, would serve as president, and George Meadows of Shreveport, Louisiana, would be the first vice president. Following the election, there was a report of the committee on con-

with a wide variety of needs. Although few results of the conference affected the private career sector, the new focus on education was refreshing.

CONSOLIDATION!

Earlier in this section we discussed the rivalry between the National Association of Accredited Commercial Schools and the newer American Association of Commercial Colleges. After the war ended, the War Emergency Council was transformed into the National Council of Business Schools, and the competition became a three-way struggle. It became obvious to most of the school leaders that something had to be done to eliminate duplication of efforts. Therefore, in 1949, it was jointly proposed that the three organizations consider consolidation into one organization with a revised structure and a new name.

The members of each organization voted on the issue, and the pre-election debates were heated. Finally, in June 1949, the Cincinnati office of Lybrand, Ross Bros. & Montgomery, Certified Public Accountants, was en-

stitution and bylaws, and a draft of these was presented and approved.

Shortly after consolidation, the officers decided that *The Business School Executive* should serve as the official publication of the Association. This periodical was formerly the voice of the NCBS, and it had been well received in the private sector. Some old-timers who remembered the publication of the first issue of *Accredited News*, back in February 1912, were saddened by this decision. Nevertheless, the new Association voice was to become a very successful professional journal for years to come.

The process of consolidation proved that the private career-school leaders were as flexible in organization matters as they were in the management of their schools. They saw the need for change and were able to break old habits to respond to new exigencies. It was not by any measure an easy thing to do, but it was the right choice. After almost forty years as the National Association of Accredited Commercial Schools, they would now be known as the National Association and Council of Business Schools (NACBS).

THE ACCREDITING COMMISSION

The word "Accredited" was dropped from the title of the consolidated organization. This is ironic since accreditation became the major item on the agenda for the National Association and Council of Business Schools in the 1950s.

Almost from the first day of its establishment, the governing board moved accreditation to the top of its priority list. Many of the Association members believed that, since the end of World War II, schools had been required to meet the needs of a much more complex and demanding pool of students. Therefore, they reasoned, it was necessary to identify more clearly the purposes and goals of each institution and the resources they had for accomplishing these goals. Many felt this process could best be accomplished through a system of accreditation. Coincidentally, the United

Typing class at Miami-Jacobs College.

States Office of Education was becoming more stringent in deciding which institutions it would recognize for participation in government-assisted programs. Private business schools had not been included in government-assisted programs because of their lack of accreditation at that time.

Jay W. Miller, President of the NACBS, wrote to the members in 1951 to solicit ideas and support for a private career-school accreditation agency. Miller stated in his message, which was published in *Business School Executive*, "Any accreditation plan worthy of the name will involve a selective process. If all schools are to be accredited, the plan isn't worth anything; the plan then becomes merely a mutual admiration society. . . . Any accreditation plan set up entirely within our own field, and limited to members of our own Association is a form of self-accreditation. This plan has worked for the high schools and the universities. . . . In any event, we must set standards with teeth in them."

By December 1952 the next president of the association, C. I. Blackwood, of Blackwood College in Oklahoma City, Oklahoma, appointed a steering committee to conduct the development of an accreditation program. This led to the establishment of the Accrediting Commission of the Association, and the appointment of

H. D. Hopkins as the first executive secretary.

An amendment to the NACBS constitution known as Amendment No. 1, Article IX, established the Accrediting Commission and the accreditation process as an integral part of the Association. The amendment stated: "The name of this organization shall be the Accrediting Commission for Business Schools (hereafter referred to as the 'Commission'). . . . The principal objective of the Accrediting Commission for Business Schools is the improvement of education among post-secondary institutions devoted largely, or exclusively, to business education."

The amendment called for the election of seven commissioners, each to be elected from a designated geographical region of the country. It was made clear that the commissioners should be separate and distinct from the Board of Directors of the Association. However, the Board did have the right to appoint "other commissioners" to the Commission for a two-year term. The commissioners were to be aided in their task by a board of examiners. The examiners were Association members and others authorized by the Commission to "investigate and inspect" those institutions desiring accreditation. The Commission was to appoint members from accredited schools for each visit, as well as "an educator of unimpeachable integrity and competence from outside the institutions accredited by the Commission." Those selected would have to be free from conflicts of interest, and act objectively.

Under Section 253 of the Veteran's Readjustment Assistance Act of 1952, the commissioner of education is required to publish a list of nationally recognized accrediting agencies and associations that he determines to be reliable. The NACBS wasted no time in applying for recognition. The Commission was successful and gained recognition. This was a giant step forward for the accreditation process and the members of the Association.

Accreditation standards were carefully developed and were constantly under scrutiny by the Commission and the Association. In 1957 these standards and practices underwent major revision. The work of revision was done by the Committee on Standards, under the direction of Harold B. Post, President of Post Junior College in Waterbury, Connecticut. Among the revised standards was one classifying schools as junior or senior colleges. The revised standards also included requirements for new faculty entering the field. The revisions required that applicants admitted to an accredited school hold a recognized high-school diploma or its equivalent. Published catalogs and minimum degree requirements were also made part of the revised standards. The revised standards and practices attempted to achieve higher quality in education, student services, and administration.

IN MEMORIAM

By 1954 the Association was forty-two years old. As with any vital organization, change was inevitable. So it was with the Association. One major change had been the replacement of *Accredited News* with *Business School Executive* as the official voice of the Association. Another change was the location of the Association's headquarters—from the office of the secretary of the organization to a permanent home in Washington, D.C., in the Howe Building.

Ben Williams, the founder of this Association, saw these and many more changes occur. He spent over fifty years in private career education, twenty-five of these as president of the Association. He continued to be active in NACBS until his death in 1954. When Williams died, Bruce F. Gates, President Emeritus of Gates College in Waterloo, Iowa, and a close friend, wrote: "Yes, Ben is gone. But his influence will go down through the years in the lives of thousands of young people who were influenced by his teaching and his character during the 50-odd years he served as teacher and president at the Capital City Commercial College in Des Moines; yes, and in the lives of hundreds of teachers and managers of business schools who drew inspiration from his life and work."

Hubert E. V. Porter, Williams's right-hand man and secretary of the Association from its inception, died eight years before Williams, in 1946, at the age of eighty-four. Almost up to the date of his death, Hubert Porter continued as secretary of the Association, although illness curtailed his activities during his final years. *Accredited News* stated that while in poor health he maintained a regular work schedule; he was fatally stricken while working one evening in his office, on March 24, 1946.

Two years after Porter's death, John Robert Gregg died, on February 23, 1948, at age eighty. *Accredited News* noted the event: "It is only proper to record the passing of Dr. Gregg and to acknowledge the great contribution he made to business education, and thus, indirectly, to American business and, for that matter, world business."

Of the many outstanding activists and friends of the Association, these three were among the greatest in its history. Their contributions and influence are still very much alive in the Association and in private career education as a whole.

UNIFICATION

At the time of consolidation the members of the American Association of Commercial Colleges decided to remain independent, and the union of the NCBS and NAACS went ahead without AACC. This merger left two major competitors where there had been three. As the NACBS grew stronger in the 1950s, and its Accrediting Commission continued in its quest for renewed quality, the AACC began having second thoughts.

In 1958 Dean C. Sweetland, President of the Southeastern Business College Association, a regional organization of private career schools, called for the unification of the AACC and the NACBS. Sweetland suggested that the combined organization be named the Federated Business College Association. He presented his proposed plan for unification to *The Compass*, the journal of the AACC, and *The Balance Sheet*, published for business educators by the South-

Typing class at Huertas Junior College, taught by founder Juan Huertas.

ern Publishing Company, in the hope that the publicity might snowball into meaningful negotiations between the two organizations. Sweetland stated: "It appears to me that the outline presents a plan which will result inevitably in an increased professional stature for all private business schools. It also provides a medium for the preservation on a permanent basis of the ideals and objectives of both the constituent groups."

Sweetland's timing was right: the members of the two private business-school associations entered into a unification agreement that took effect on May 5, 1962. The name of the new unified association was the United Business Schools Association (UBSA), and its headquarters was at 1518 K Street, in Washington, D.C. Weldon L. Strawn, of Massey Business College in Houston, was named as the first president of UBSA, and former officers of both NACBS and AACC served with him on the new board of directors. Other officers of the Association included Harold B. Post, of Post Junior College of Commerce in Waterbury, Connecticut; Jack H. Jones, of Jones Business College in Jacksonville, Florida; Walter J. Tribbey, of Draughon School of Business in Tulsa, Oklahoma; and G. C. Stewart, of Draughon's Business College in

The COMPASS

Official Publication of the UNITED BUSINESS SCHOOLS ASSOCIATION

| VOLUME 26 | WASHINGTON, D.C., MAY, 1962 | NUMBER 5 |

UNIFICATION!

Reprinted from The Compass.

Lubbock, Texas. The president-elect was Hugh T. Barnes, of Barnes School of Business in Denver.

It was decided that the Association should have a full-time permanent executive director. Richard A. Fulton became executive director and general counsel of UBSA. And *The Compass* became the official voice of the Association. *The Business School Executive* ceased publication.

The May 1962 issue of *The Compass* applauded unification: "Two competing associations have at times created confusion in the minds of the people with whom they would be educational partners. Others have found in this competition an excuse for neutrality and non-competition. Now, with one strong association spending all of its energies working for the good of the industry, private business schools are, in fact, becoming partners in the nation's educational programs and in the planning for the future."

At the time of unification, the UBSA represented almost five hundred private business schools, with total enrollments of over 150,000 students. This was a decrease in the number of members that the separate associations had served in earlier years. Over the years, the growth of the public sector of career education had taken its toll on private business school enrollments.

The consolidation of NAACS and the NCBS in 1950 had paved the way for the later unification with AACC.

The most significant result of the consolidation was the establishment of the Accrediting Commission and its subsequent recognition by the United States Commissioner of Education. The success of the Accrediting Commission was one of the main reasons that the AACC merged with NACBS.

GOLDEN ANNIVERSARY CELEBRATION

"Partners in Progress" was the theme of the first convention of the NACBS. The theme emphasized the fifty-year partnership between private business schools and the private sector and reflected the Association's hopes for developing new partners from outside the Association. Some of those identified included the American Personnel and Guidance Association, the United States Civil Service Commission, and the National Association of Secondary Schools. In the spirit of fostering future alliances, speakers from these organizations were invited to participate in the convention.

The fiftieth birthday was celebrated at the Shoreham Hotel in Washington, D.C., on November 1–2, 1962. During this first convention "behind the unified organization," it was emphasized that within the Association "lies a history of fifty years of independent private business school cooperation through some type of organized activity."

A distinguished group of speakers was featured at the celebration. At the November 1 afternoon session, John W. Macy, Jr., Chairman of the United States Civil Service Commission, addressed the delegates. Macy discussed the changing graduation requirements and various testing methods. The keynote speaker at the convention was Dr. Thomas N. Carroll, President of George Washington University. Dr. Ellsworth Tompkins, Executive Secretary of the National Association of Secondary School Principals, was also on the program. Entertainment at the celebration was provided by Chester Lauk, also known as "Lum" of "Lum n' Abner" fame. (How many of you recall this well-known radio situation comedy, which played for several decades?)

Public relations was becoming an exciting new field in the early 1960s, and the members were interested in knowing more about it. To this end, Harold Leffel, the Director of Public Relations for Kinman Business University in Spokane, Washington, conducted a workshop at the convention. And Carl McDaniels, Associate Director of the American Personnel and Guidance Association, addressed the general session on the role of counselors in private career schools.

The flavor of this golden anniversary celebration was quite different from that of the silver anniversary convention in 1937. Though the fiftieth anniversary had some light moments, the pervading feeling was that there was much work to be done, and the program focused on the most vital of those tasks. Of immediate importance were the present needs of the collective member schools. Therefore, a series of "how-to" lectures and workshops were held for interested educators and administrators. People spoke of the possibilities for future membership growth, and the challenges the private sector of education would face. In contrast, the twenty-fifth anniversary convention had been more of a nostalgic celebration, a gathering of old friends recalling the past.

The dynamic composition of the new organization, with participants from so many different backgrounds, surely must have been fascinating. They were

Accounting class at Draughon's Business College.

together celebrating fifty years of association, yet some hardly knew one another, and it was their first meeting as a unified body. In previous years, the two associations often met at the same time and place, but in different conclaves. From all accounts, the convention was a great success and helped launch UBSA as one of the most effective and visible associations of its kind in the country.

INSIDE AND OUT

Only those who had lived through the period could truly appreciate the enormous changes that took place on both sides of the school door between 1937 and 1962. Outside, the economy had shifted from depressed, to government controlled, to consumer driven. Moreover, the American emotional life moved from the fear for survival, all the way over to the need for personal growth. Inside the classroom, the broad spectrum of "learning to earn" opportunities exploded, and the rise of new technologies challenged educators.

The internal environment of the Association had gone through enormous changes as well. The difficulties of inadequate representation of the private-career school sector had finally been resolved. The process of accreditation had become a vital activity, as witnessed by the recognition of the Accrediting Commission by federal and state agencies. With the turmoil of the past quarter century finally behind them, the Association leaders and member schools were ready to move on to new frontiers.

Chapter 5
Prospecting for a Diamond
(1962–1987)

It is the year in which Algeria becomes an independent nation, Georges Pompidou becomes premier of France, and the Soviet Union establishes an unmistakable presence in Cuba, promising future arms shipments to support the Castro regime. In the United States, the civil rights of blacks are challenged as James Meredith, a black applicant, is denied admission to the University of Mississippi by Governor Barnett. The United States Court of Appeals finds Barnett guilty of civil contempt, yet it takes United States marshalls and 3,000 soldiers to suppress riots when Meredith arrives on campus to begin classes.

From the White House, John F. Kennedy appoints Byron White and Arthur Goldberg to the United States Supreme Court. United States astronauts rocket into headlines with feats formerly in the realm of science fiction. John Glenn becomes the first American to orbit the earth. In separate flights, astronauts Scott Carpenter and Wally Schirra also venture into space. Back on terra firma, the Royal College of Physicians issues a shocking report on smoking and health. The world is saddened by the deaths of Eleanor Roosevelt, Charles Laughton, and Marilyn Monroe.

Edward Albee's first full-length play, *Who's Afraid of Virginia Woolf?*, shocks Broadway audiences with its devastating portrait of an American marriage. A crusading biologist, Rachel Carson, aims a crushing blow at the multimillion-dollar pesticide industry with the publication of *Silent Spring* in which she argued that certain pesticides could "still the song of birds . . . " and, indeed, threaten human beings as well. Frank Loesser and Abe Burrows win a Pulitzer Prize for their hit show *How to Succeed in Business Without Really Trying*. John Steinbeck receives the Nobel Prize for Literature for his nonfiction best-seller *Travels with Charley: In Search of America*. *Lawrence of Arabia* is the big winner at the Academy Awards ceremony.

The New York Yankees win the World Series again, squeaking by the San Francisco Giants four games to three. In England, Arnold Palmer

Secretarial students taking dictation at Robinson Business College.

wins his second straight British Open Golf Championship. Palmer also wins the Master's Tournament for the third time. In college football, Minnesota defeats UCLA by a score of 21-3 to win the Rose Bowl.

This was the setting in which the Association celebrated its golden anniversary. The Association, finally consolidated, moved on to its fifty-first year of operation with a new name: United Business Schools Association (UBSA).

HISTORICAL PERSPECTIVE

The postwar baby boom resulted in a huge number of teenagers and young adults by 1962. Many of these young people grew up in middle-class homes where education was considered an important part of the maturation process. By surrounding himself with some of the leading intellectuals from the nation's most prestigious universities, President John F. Kennedy seemed to reinforce this way of thinking. Kennedy's "brain trust" helped emphasize the importance of obtaining a good education. At the other end of the spectrum, though, were many whites, blacks, and Hispanics who had little chance and few opportunities to get a quality education.

Americans were shocked by the news that the Soviet Union had successfully launched a satellite, Sputnik I, into space. The Soviet space program, it was apparent, was ahead of the American space program. Americans

immediately began to reexamine curricula in science, mathematics, and engineering. A concerted effort was made to identify students with potential in these areas and to provide them with enriched learning experiences. President Kennedy pledged to the world that Americans would walk on the moon; although he did not live to see it, his promise was fulfilled in 1969.

The 1960s were marked by discontent, unrest, and upheaval. Many things contributed to the increasing gap between the suburban middle class and the urban poor. Among these were the assassinations of John F. Kennedy, Malcolm X, Martin Luther King, Jr., and Robert F. Kennedy; intense civil rights activism; and growing disenchantment with the Vietnam War. Young people were especially feverish in their determination to change the system. Social activism frequently took the forms of riots, bombings, and murders. In short, it was an extremely unsettled and unsettling period.

By 1973 the Vietnam conflict was behind us, but troubles still lingered on. Americans had to face up to many harsh realities. We began to feel the sting of foreign competition. We suffered through several oil crises, which threatened major industries dependent on this vital source of energy. In addition, those areas of the nation that had become dependent on domestic oil and natural gas revenues were hard hit by the shortages and ensuing inflation.

In the 1970s women became more militant in their quest for equality. They expressed the need for equal recognition and equal pay in the workplace. The family has gone through a restructuring as a result of the new role of women in society. Average family sizes have decreased dramatically over the past quarter century, and today there are many single-person households and a new subculture composed of yuppies (young urban professionals) and dinks (double income, no kids). Such changes have had a pronounced impact on our society and economy.

Although civil rights issues, political scandals, social welfare problems, and world tensions have dominated headlines over the last twenty-five years, technology has advanced rapidly and with relatively little fanfare. In the forefront of this technological advancement is the computer. The first computers were mechanical giants, working slowly and deliberately. Prototypes were soon scaled down to a more reasonable size, operating speeds increased, and capabilities multiplied. Finally, convenient desktop computers have emerged, opening up the industry to an ever-increasing number of users. As computers have become commonplace in businesses, in schools, and at home, fear of their mystical powers has diminished.

Progress in science and health care has been astounding over the past twenty-five years. Antibiotics are routinely used to treat a host of ailments. Coronary bypass surgery, organ transplants, and other advanced surgical procedures are being performed every day. Diagnostic equipment, such as the CAT scan, have become critical tools in many medical procedures, and hospitals often find it difficult to keep up with the latest advances.

The past twenty-five years have given us an enormous assortment of new consumer products and services. Television added color, remote control, wide screens, and stereophonic sound. Compact disc players, which use lasers to "read" the grooves in discs, are becoming the standard in high-fidelity sound. Our stomachs and palates have survived fast-food fads, microwave mania, and, more recently, take-out fever. For our business and personal travel, we now have superhighways and fast-moving commercial jets; like the parts of a working machine, everyone seems to be in constant motion. The United States consumer convenience craze has had no parallel in the history of the world.

Progress is not without hardships, however. The oil crisis, for example, contributed to a depressed economy. Foreign goods and foreign investments continue to cause great concern in our domestic markets. Inflation, the rise and fall of the dollar, as well as fluctuating interest rates, are all constant causes for worry. Furthermore, the decay of many industries in the large urban centers of the Northeast and Midwest have left many Americans unemployed.

Dictation lab at Parks School of Business.

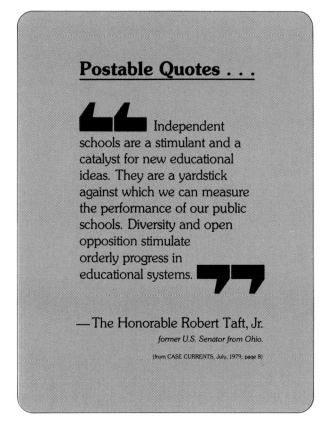

Postable Quotes . . .

" Independent schools are a stimulant and a catalyst for new educational ideas. They are a yardstick against which we can measure the performance of our public schools. Diversity and open opposition stimulate orderly progress in educational systems. "

— The Honorable Robert Taft, Jr.
former U.S. Senator from Ohio.

(from CASE CURRENTS, July, 1979, page 8)

Reprinted from AICS Compass.

The Fab Four revolutionized the sounds of
rock 'n' roll.

London's top model Twiggy, in a mini-
dress. Believe it or not, those hemlines are
back.

Artist's concept of the docking approach of
an American Apollo spacecraft to a Soviet
Soyuz spacecraft.

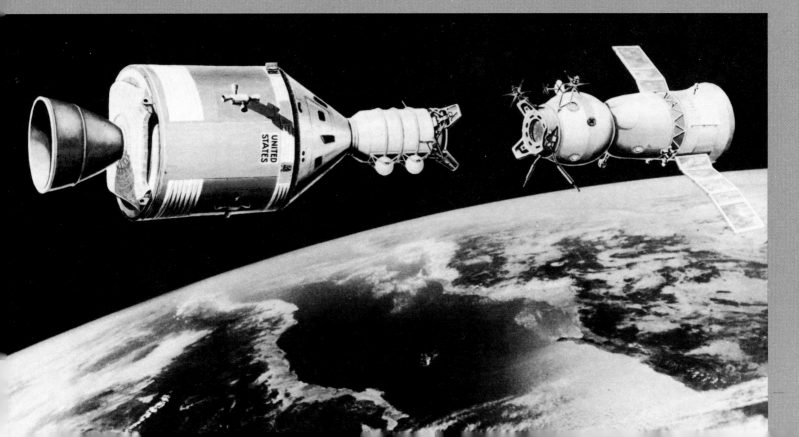

Civil rights marchers, led by Dr. Martin Luther King, Jr., on their way to Montgomery, Alabama.

Dr. Christiaan Barnard explaining the operation he performed—transplanting the heart of a fatally injured girl to a man with an impaired heart.

John F. Kennedy at work in the Oval Office.

Anti-war protestors at the Pentagon in 1970.

President Nixon at the Great Wall of China.

With his wife seated behind him, John Dean begins his testimony before the Senate Watergate Committee.

President Jimmy Carter arranged the historic meeting between Menachem Begin and Anwar Sadat at Camp David in 1978.

Freed American hostages arrive from Iran in United States Air Force medical rescue plane.

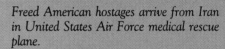

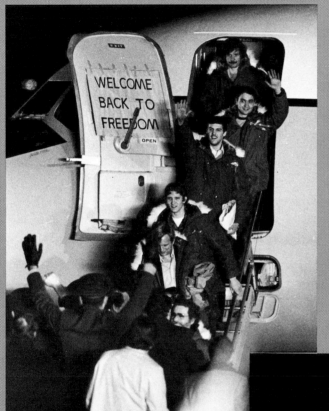

Ronald Reagan gives the thumbs-up sign at Los Angeles election headquarters.

Sixty years after receiving the right to vote, women march in support of the Equal Rights Amendment.

Walter Mondale, in a historic decision, selects Geraldine Ferraro to be his running mate.

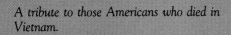

A tribute to those Americans who died in Vietnam.

grams offered by these institutions had become so complex that the former name was no longer completely descriptive of the member institutions of the Association.

The resolution also proposed that the title of the Accrediting Commission for Business Schools (ACBS) be changed to the Accrediting Commission. Again, the more varied nature of the programs within the schools was the primary motivation for this action. Both actions were adopted by the membership.

This was the first change in the Association's name since the UBSA was formed in 1962 as a result of the merger of the National Association and Council of Business Schools and the American Association of Commercial Colleges. It marked the fourth time in its sixty-year history that the Association had changed its name. Still, as William Shakespeare put it in *Romeo and Juliet*: "A rose by any other name would smell as sweet."

The Association changed its location, too. The UBSA moved into the Madison National Bank Building at 1730 M Street, N.W., Washington, D.C., in June 1969. On June 1, 1983, AICS moved their offices from that M Street location to the National Center for Higher Education Building at Dupont Circle. As stated in *AICS Compass*, "this address has become synonymous with higher education nationally and is perhaps the best known throughout the educational community."

ON CAPITOL HILL

The establishment of a Washington, D.C., office was a giant step forward for the Association. The new address created a host of opportunities for continuous interaction with Congress, government agencies, and affiliated organizations. The combination of the move to Washington and the addition of a full-time professional staff enabled the Association to become the dynamic and responsive voice of the membership on Capitol Hill that it is.

In 1964 the Association held the UBSA Capitol Conference to discuss

The first student in the Johnson & Wales culinary division being fitted for his uniform.

WHAT KIND OF A MEMBER ARE YOU?

Some members are like wheelbarrows —no good unless pushed.

Some are like canoes—they need to be paddled.

Some are like kites—if you don't keep string on them they will blow away.

Some are like footballs—you can't tell which way they are going to bounce.

Some are like balloons—full of wind and likely to blow up unless handled carefully.

Some are like trailers—no good unless pulled.

Some are 100% members in regular attendance at meetings and are very cooperative—are you one of these?

—From The Compass

Rhode Island Governor Frank Licht grants authority to Johnson & Wales College to award baccalaureate degrees. With Governor Licht are Morris Gaebe (left) and Jack Yena (right).

the Vocational Education Act. Robert W. Sneden, President of UBSA and Davenport College in Grand Rapids, Michigan, opened the conference on May 18 by exhorting the delegates to assist Congress by offering their school facilities to state education officials to train people for jobs.

Representatives of member schools from thirty-five states attended the Capitol Conference. Many special guests also attended, including Dr. M.D. Mobley, Executive Secretary of the American Vocational Association, and Drs. Edwin L. Rumpf and Bruce I. Blackstone, specialists for Vocational and Technical Education at the United States Office of Education of the Department of Health, Education and Welfare (HEW). Dr. Walter M. Arnold, Assistant Commissioner of the United States Office of Education, was the speaker at the noon luncheon of the conference. It was one of the first of many significant events to be hosted by the Association in Washington.

In 1965 the UBSA received landmark recognition when President Lyndon Johnson invited Robert Sneden and Executive Director Richard Fulton to the White House to attend the signing of additional amendments to the National Defense Education Act. These amendments provided significant educational benefits to veterans of the Vietnam War. Sneden received from President Johnson a pen that was used to sign the document into law.

Around this same era, two other federal laws that affected private career schools were proposed. The Economic Opportunity Act of 1964 (Public Law 88-452) authorized the expenditure of $950 million for vocational education by the Job Corps for the 1964–1965 fiscal year. The UBSA was successful in urging that "both local educational agencies and private vocational educational institutions" be included in the Act. The second piece of legislation of vital importance to the private career sector was the War Orphans Educational Assistance Act (Public Law 83-361). This Act included private career schools among those eligible to provide education paid for by government grants to children of totally and permanently disabled veterans, as well as to the children of war widows.

The UBSA fought hard to be included under the Manpower Development Training Act (MDTA). In 1967 the Association was invited to participate in an MDTA demonstration project through a contract with the Department of Health, Education and Welfare and the Office of Education. Under this project, funds totaling $300,000 were allocated for the training of about 450 people from eight states. Institutions participating in the program included trade and technical schools and business schools with trade and technical divisions. Captain Eugene W. Davis, a retired United States Navy officer, was appointed assistant executive director of the MDTA project. Opportunities for private career schools were further expanded under this program.

In the mid 1970s, Basic Educational Opportunity Grants (later renamed Pell Grants) became available to postsecondary students. Under this legislation, an eligible student could receive between $200 and $1,400 per year to help pay for educational expenses, and the government did not require repayment of these awards. Student eligibility was based on financial need, and the grants could be applied to tuition in private career schools as well as in academic institutions.

The Pell Grant, as well as the Guaranteed Student Loan Program, opened educational doors to many financially disadvantaged students. Because so many students wanted quick access to quality employment situations, many chose to enroll in private career schools. These acts prompted a renewed interest in the learning-to-earn movement.

Another major boost to enrollments came from the influx of veterans who qualified for educational benefits under the G.I. Bill. In 1976, a record 2.2 million persons were enrolled under the provisions of the G.I. Bill, and from 1966–1976, 6.5 million veterans and service people received some form of training as a result of their service in the armed forces. Although exact figures are not available, it is believed that several hundred thousand veterans attended private vocational institutions during this period, and many were enrolled in AICS schools.

It is hardly news to most school administrators that an understanding of complex government regulations is essential to the effective management of schools. In the 1970s, Congress passed several complicated and important regulations. The Family Educational Rights and Privacy Act of 1974, known as the Buckley Amendment, has had a significant impact on the way schools communicate. Another of these, the Rehabilitation Act of 1973, Section 504, called for access capabilities for the disabled. In addition, the Rehabilitation Act resulted in increased opportunities for facilities management in educational institutions. Regulations by the United States Immigration and Naturalization Service regarding foreign students enrolled in United States schools also affected private career school administrators.

Quite a controversy developed between the private career sector and the Federal Trade Commission (FTC) in the mid 1970s. The issues were complex; basically the FTC wanted to impose a special set of restrictions on proprietary schools regarding refund policies and other consumer practices. The issues were heard in the federal courts but never completely resolved to the satisfaction of private school administrators.

In 1985 AICS recommended to Congress that legislative changes be

GOING BACK TO SCHOOL AT 35

One of 50 men and women age 35 and over are using their leisure time to go "back to school." Many are studying to keep up with new developments in their chosen field or to obtain the credentials necessary to enter a different line of work. Some are housewives taking college courses to obtain an undergraduate degree before reentering the labor market. Others are workers seeking a high school diploma or college degree in response to rising employer hiring and promotion requirements.

—*From* The Compass

Dictation class at Parks School of Business.

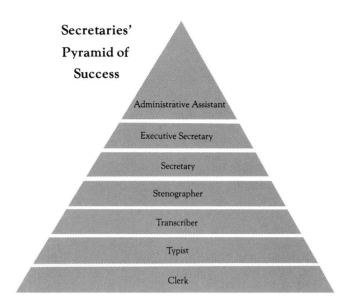

Secretaries'
Pyramid of
Success

Administrative Assistant

Executive Secretary

Secretary

Stenographer

Transcriber

Typist

Clerk

Reprinted from International Business College catalog.

Personal Qualification
for Secretaries

Initiative
Responsibility
Oral and written communication skills
Ability to supervise
Maturity
Organizational skills
Positive attitude

—From The International
Business College catalog

made to the Higher Education Act. The Association called for increased private career school access to federally sponsored programs. It also encouraged the continued role of federal government in all postsecondary education. The AICS general counsel, William Clohan, stated, "Our main concern is to ensure that the final bill helps provide the opportunities for all Americans to acquire the skills necessary to obtain steady and productive employment." This is a good example of the constant efforts of the Association to lobby Congress in the interests of member schools and private career education as a whole.

Also in 1985, Congress passed a resolution, signed into law by President Reagan, that directed the Department of Defense to provide tuition reimbursements to service personnel attending institutions accredited by an agency recognized by the Secretary of Education and the Council on Postsecondary Education. This action allowed service personnel attending AICS institutions to receive tuition reimbursements. This resulted in an additional boost in enrollments in private career schools. Dr. Jerry W. Miller, President of AICS, noted that "Most of the skills our institutions teach are directly applicable to military jobs. . . . We look forward to working with education officials in the military in implementing the Congressional mandate and are pleased that private career schools and colleges will now be able to serve all military personnel."

These are several examples of how active the Association has been on Capitol Hill in the past quarter century.

MEMBERS IN SERVICE TO THE NATION

The Association's new awareness of its role on Capitol Hill led to increased activity. Association representatives, many of whom were already active in Association affairs, became more confident about participating in Washington affairs. As a result, they were frequently asked to serve on federal boards, committees, and affiliated national associations. This recognition increased the enthusiasm of members and the fine reputation of AICS.

Jay W. Miller, an active member of the Association since the 1930s, was appointed for several terms to the Veterans Administration Advisory Council. Miller, President of Goldey Beacom School of Business in Wilmington, Delaware (now known as Goldey Beacom College), participated in the council's activities from 1957–1966 and became a respected figure on the Washington education scene as a result of his distinguished service.

In 1966 President Johnson announced the appointments of Minnie L. Gaston, of the Booker T. Washington Business College in Birmingham, Alabama, and Dr. John E. Binnion, Professor of Education at Texas Tech and a member of the AICS Accrediting Commission, to an eight-member advisory council on insured loans for vocational students. The council was established under the National Vocational Student Loan Insurance Act of 1965 and was intended to encourage loan insurance programs for students seeking training in business, trade, and technical and other vocational schools.

In 1968, The National Commission on Accrediting, forerunner of the Council on Postsecondary Education (COPA), appointed former UBSA President Harry G. Green to its Council on Occupational Education. Green was one of fifteen members on the council. Membership consisted of state and local education officials, state university administrators, and public and private vocational school educators. This appointment was an important act of recognition of Green and the Accrediting Commission of UBSA.

In 1969, G.C. Stewart, Director of Draughon's Business College in Lubbock, Texas, and Chairman of the Accrediting Commission of UBSA, was appointed to the United States Office of Education's Advisory Council on Financial Aid. This was a significant appointment because it provided the Association with a direct link to the important activities of the Office of Education.

Former AICS President Morris J.W. Gaebe became a member of the Board of Directors of the Student Loan Marketing Association in 1973. Gaebe was one of seven educators named to the twenty-one member board, known as the Sallie Mae Corporation. This corporation was authorized by Congress to administer the secondary market for student loans. Gaebe, President of Johnson & Wales College in Providence, Rhode Island, was subsequently appointed to the Executive Committee of the Board as well.

A. R. Sullivan, President of Sullivan Junior College of Business, was the first private career school administrator appointed to the board of directors of the American Council on Education.

The Secretary of Health, Education and Welfare, Caspar W. Weinberger, appointed Jack H. Jones, past chairman of the AICS Accrediting Commission and President of Jones College in Jacksonville, Florida, to the HEW Advisory Council on Financial Aid for a term beginning on June 30, 1974. The council's purpose was to advise the Commissioner of Education on matters of policy relating to financial assistance programs for students, and to evaluate the effectiveness of these programs. The twenty-one–member council submitted an annual report of its activities to Congress.

Also in 1974, Ernest Roblee, outgoing chairman of the Accrediting Commission and President of Jamestown Business College in Jamestown,

Basketball at New Hampshire College.

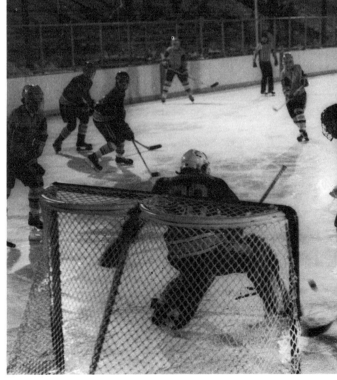

Hockey at New Hampshire College.

First class of culinary arts students at Johnson & Wales.

New York, was appointed to the board of the newly formed Council on Postsecondary Accreditation.

In the final days of the Carter administration, Shirley Hufstedler, Secretary of Education, appointed Jan Eisenhour Friedheim to the National Advisory Committee on Accreditation and Institutional Eligibility. Jan Friedheim, former chairman of the AICS Board of Directors, was later reappointed to the National Advisory Committee by Education Secretary Terrel Bell. Other appointees to this committee were William Meadows, President of Meadows College in Columbus, Georgia, and Norine Fuller, Executive Director of Financial Aid at the Fashion Institute of Design and Marketing in Los Angeles, California.

In addition to serving on various boards and committees, AICS members have actively testified on Capitol Hill and participated in programs of national organizations. Joe E. Lee, President-elect of AICS in 1976, chaired a session at the Thirty-first Conference on Higher Education in Chicago, on March 9, 1976. In 1985, Mary Ann Lawlor, a member of the AICS Board, testified before Congress on the consequences of the Reagan budget. These are a few of the ways in which individual Association members have served the nation.

PROFESSIONAL STAFF

After the merger that established the UBSA, an effort was made to engage and maintain a full-time professional staff in the Washington, D.C., head-

quarters. In 1961 the Board appointed attorney Richard Fulton to serve as Executive Director and General Counsel of the Association. Before his appointment, Fulton had served in Louisiana as an attorney and later worked as administrative assistant to United States Senator Allen J. Ellender. Fulton served as Executive Director until 1976, when he left to pursue his private practice, but he remained as General Counsel until 1982, when he was succeeded by William C. Clohan, Jr.

The new Executive Director appointed by the Board in 1976 was Stephen B. Friedheim. Friedheim came to AICS after serving as Executive Vice President of the American Society for Medical Technology (ASMT) and as the Executive Director of the ASMT Education and Research Fund, Inc. Although this organization was based in Houston, Texas, Friedheim knew his way around Capitol Hill. He had previously lived and worked in Washington, D.C., when he was Director of Public Relations and Assistant to the Executive Director of the American Personnel and Guidance Association.

In 1978, the title of Executive Director was changed to President of the Association. The title of Chairman of the Board would now be used to designate the highest elected official of the organization. The position of President, formerly known as Chairman of the Board, would be filled by an outside person hired by the Board of Directors. Henceforth, the duties of the President of the Association would be to oversee all staff operations.

Friedheim served until 1984. In his statement to the Executive Committee of the Board, he said, "When I was hired in 1976, there were certain goals I set for myself which were approved by the Board. We have more than met those objectives. I owe that success to each of the Boards for which I have served and each of the Accrediting Commissions which have been selected in those years. We have a great staff . . . I think the best in Washington!"

After a fourteen-week nationwide search for a new President, the Board selected Dr. Jerry W. Miller. Charles Palmer, Chairman of the Board, stated, "We are pleased to announce Dr. Miller's selection from over 300 resumes. He is the ideal choice for this position." Miller had previously served as Vice President for Academic Affairs and Institutional Relations for the American Council on Education (ACE). He didn't have very far to travel to get to his new job, however, since both organizations were located in the National Center for Higher Education. More than 150 guests gathered at the Phillips Art Gallery in Washington on August 7, 1984, to bid farewell to Stephen Friedheim and to welcome Jerry Miller.

Dr. James R. Taylor served as Secretary of the Accrediting Commission for Business Schools during its first six years under the UBSA banner. Upon his retirement, UBSA President G.C. Stewart paid Taylor the following tribute: "During the service of Dr. James R. Taylor we have seen mounting evidence of the increased professional acceptance of ACBS accreditation. The revised system of accreditation procedures remains a lasting monument to the efforts of Jim Taylor . . ."

In June 1969, Dana R. Hart, a former ACBS commissioner and UBSA director, resigned as director of Durham Business College in Pasadena, Texas, to accept the position of ACBS executive secretary. Hart had attended Texas Wesleyan College and received his M.S. degree from North Texas State University. Association members and friends were shocked when Dana Hart died suddenly on March 17, 1977. Richard Fulton offered a memorable tribute to Dana Hart at the 1977 AICS convention in San Francisco: "It is an intimidating experience for me to speak about Dana R. Hart. This is not only because he was a dear friend, an esteemed colleague, in fact a partner in the affairs of AICS and its Accrediting Commission, but because I can still see that humorous twinkle in his eyes fastened on me, the patient understanding smile. . . . Once that look of Dana's is fixed on you, you cannot be stuffy, you cannot be untrue and, moreover, you cannot be unfair."

In 1976 Sanford-Brown College placed fifteen finalists in the Phi Beta Lambda (Future Business Leaders of America) Spring Leadership Conference.

The Dana R. Hart Memorial Research Grant

The Dana R. Hart Memorial Research Grant was established in 1977 in order to stimulate, encourage, and reward outstanding contributions to the field of independent career education.

1978	*Dr. Mary M. Blyth* *Detroit College of Business*
1979	*Mr. Donald E. Schaeffer* *Condie College*
1980	*Dr. Wellford W. "Buzz" Wilms* *University of California*
1981	*Ms. Marci L. Cox* *University of California*
1982	*Dr. Jerry Kokalis, Jr.* *E.A. Henry School of Business*
1983	*Dr. Irving Schneider* *Johnson & Wales College*
1984	*Dr. Gail Hentz Laoria* *Roberts-Walsh Business School*
1985	*Dr. Cheryl Anne Fell* *Cheryl Fell's School of Business*
1986	*Dr. Jack R. Jones* *The Berkeley Schools*

Robert M. Toren, a member of the Association staff, was appointed Executive Secretary of the Accrediting Commission at a meeting of the Board in May 1977. Toren resigned in 1979 and went into private career school administration. Prentiss Carnell III, AICS Board chairman, noted: "In the time he has served the Commission we have benefited from his advice and leadership."

Dr. James M. Phillips succeeded Toren with the new title of Executive Director of the Accrediting Commission. Dr. Phillips received his Ph.D. from Catholic University of America and had previously served as staff associate for the Council on Postsecondary Accreditation in Washington, D.C. Prentiss Carnell said of Phillips' appointment, "We wanted to be assured that our opportunities to grow and develop would be enhanced through the assistance and guidance of effective staff. In Jim Phillips we have such a person."

Sue Berke King, Vice President of Administration and Finance for AICS, recently received special recognition. In March 1986, Board members and Association staff gathered to celebrate King's twentieth anniversary with AICS.

Sue King celebrates twenty years at AICS with (left to right) Richard Fulton, Jerry Miller, and Edward Shapiro.

AUTHORS

Many of the Association's members and professional staff are authors of books and articles on career education. One of the most prominant of these, Dr. Jay W. Miller, was one of the most active members in the seventy-five–year history of the Association. Dr. Miller, President of Goldey Beacom School of Business in Wilmington, Delaware, along with Dr. William J. Hamilton of the Pierce School of Business Administration in Philadelphia, co-authored *The Independent Business School in American Education.* Published by the McGraw-Hill Book Company in 1964, this book was the most definitive text of the time on private career education.

Charles E. Palmer, an Association activist for several decades, thought that, like so many other educators, he'd like to write a book. And he did just that! Along with Robert H. Van Voorhis and Fred C. Archer, Palmer co-authored *College Accounting Theory and Practice.* The book was published by the Gregg Division of McGraw-Hill Book Company in 1963 while Palmer, a certified public accountant, was serving as President of four Palmer Colleges and as Vice Chairman of the Accrediting Commission (ACBS) of the UBSA.

Dr. Charles G. Reigner of the H.M. Rowe Company was an associate of the organization for many years. Reigner, a prolific author, wrote many articles in Association publications. His most noted work was *Beginnings of the Business School.*

E.O. Fenton, an active Association member, wrote several articles over the years for the Association publications. One article published in *The Business School Executive* in September 1957 was titled "Higher Education for All Without Taxation." At the time of this article, Fenton was President Emeritus of the American Institute of Business in Des Moines, Iowa. C.C. Steed, President of Elizabethton School of Business in Elizabethton, Tennessee, was also a frequent guest author in Association publications. One of his articles appeared in the April 1945 issue of *Accredited News* and was titled "Private Business Schools in the Light of a New Day."

Another active member of the Association for many years, A.G. Gaston of Booker T. Washington Junior

College, wrote a very interesting account of his life and times. The book, *Green Power*, was originally published by the A.G. Gaston Boys' Club in 1968. This autobiographical volume was reprinted by Troy State University Press in 1977.

AICS staff members have also written numerous articles over the years, and many have contributed to textbook publications. For example, Dr. Jerry W. Miller, current President of the AICS, contributed a twenty-one page chapter to *The Nature and Integrity of the Baccalaureate Degree.* This new book is published by the American Council on Education Macmillan Series on Higher Education. Another staff author is Mary B. Wine, Director of Professional Relations for AICS. Wine is co-author of a textbook titled *College English—Grammar and Style,* published by the Gregg Division of the McGraw-Hill Book Company in 1967.

ADVANCES IN ACCREDITATION

As the years have passed, the accreditation process has become more refined. Fortunately, the Accrediting Commission has had strong leadership since its inception in the early 1950s. This leadership encouraged mutually beneficial relationships with peer groups in the educational community. Recognition by the Department of Education and a good working relationship with the Council on Postsecondary Accreditation have helped the Accrediting Commission achieve its current status. Its quest for quality education and student services has been, and continues to be, its primary mission.

Major criteria changes were enacted by the Commission in 1970. These changes were the result of an eighteen-month effort by the commissioners and the AICS membership to refine the accreditation process. The basic intent of the criteria remained unchanged, but certain significant revisions were made. Perhaps the most significant of these was a restructuring of the Commission into two councils: the Council on Business Schools and

Photographer-author-director Gordon Parks discusses his work with Brooks Institute students.

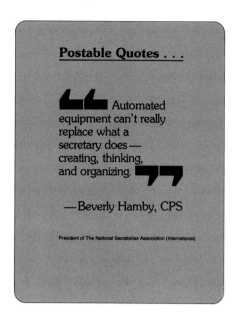
Reprinted from AICS Compass.

Council on Colleges. This restructuring did not, however, change in any way the authority of the Commission as the accrediting agency. Another important change involved the weekly teaching load requirements for business schools, junior colleges, and senior colleges. A third change mandated that the evaluation cycle for accredited schools should not exceed six years, and a new rule regarding the size of evaluation teams was instituted. In curriculum areas, guidelines for data processing courses and general education requirements were established.

The Commission established guidelines for the form and content of the financial reports of the member schools. The guidelines required initial applicants and reaccreditation applicants to submit financial reports certified by an independent certified public accountant, CPA. Further, it was decided that the CPA should have "no fiduciary or ownership affiliation with the school."

Another revision was made at the Commission meeting in April 1975; it provided "recognized candidate status" for certain institutions that are being reclassified. For example, this would apply to an accredited business school applying for a change of status from business school to junior college. The change in the criteria, Section 3-1-904, read as follows: "If the Commission, after reevaluating the institution, determines to its satisfaction that there is a reasonable assurance of reclassification when measured by these criteria, the Commission may accord the institution the status of Recognized Candidate."

In 1979 the Commission established an advisory committee that met for the first time on August 21 in Washington, D.C. The chairman of the advisory committee was Dr. Jerry Miller, who was not yet affiliated with the Association. Other members of the committee included Dr. Allison Zezulka of the University of Texas; Dr. Dorothy Peterson, a consultant for COPA; Dr. Barry Feldman, a practicing dentist; and Mrs. Carol Henderson, a graduate of the Executive Secretarial School in Dallas, Texas. In addition to the advisory committee members, the first meeting was attended by Commission Chairman, Prentiss Carnell III; Executive Director-Designate, Dr. James Phillips; Assistant Executive Director, Victor Biebighauser; Director of Education, Mary Draper; and General Counsel, Richard Fulton.

In 1981 the Commission proposed that the number of commissioners be increased. The Commission asked the membership to amend the bylaws to allow the appointment of a public commissioner to serve on the accrediting body. The change increased the number of non-Association commissioners serving on the Commission. They come from the traditional sectors of public and private higher education.

STUDENT ACTIVITIES

Most of the fraternities and sororities in member schools had faded away by the 1950s. Veterans, who comprised a large portion of the student enrollments after World War II, the Korean War, and the Vietnam War, were not exactly the fraternity or sorority type. However, a few fraternities and sororities survived through the 1960s. One of these was Alpha Iota, an honorary business sorority that was still active in 1967 when it held its twenty-second international convention at the Pfister Hotel in Milwaukee. Nearly three hundred members of Alpha Iota attended the convention; some delegates traveled from as far away as Hawaii.

Sports had become popular at several AICS schools in the 1960s and 1970s. Sullivan Business College in Louisville, for example, won its second straight NLCAA (National Little College Athletic Association) basketball championship in March 1968, in Youngstown, Ohio. The NLCAA consisted of business, technical, and two- and four-year colleges throughout the country. Schools in the NLCAA generally had enrollments under 1,000 students, with less than 500 male students. It was quite a triumph for the Sullivan team to win this title two years in succession, but they also went on to win an unprecedented third NLCAA basketball championship in 1969!

No history of American business schools would be complete without mentioning the women's basketball team of the Nashville Business College. Playing in a national collegiate women's league, under the auspices of the United States Amateur Athletic Union, the Nashville Business College team won several national and international championships during the 1940s, 1950s, and 1960s. Accompanied by their college president, H.O. Balls, the women played in Rio de Janeiro, Moscow, and several European cities.

In 1978, Fort Lauderdale College in Florida began its first football season, and, according to *National Education* magazine, was the first business college in the country to have a varsity football team. Appropriately, the name of the team was the Seagulls. They played on the road as well as at home during their first season. In 1981, Fort Lauderdale College was accepted into the National Association of Intercollegiate Athletics (NAIA), and plans were made to institute teams in baseball and soccer. Colleges accepted by the NAIA had to be accredited by COPA-recognized accrediting agencies.

In September 1983, *AICS Compass* (the name was changed in September 1976 from *The Compass*) reported that the Alpha Beta Kappa Honor Society was experiencing a rapid growth among AICS schools and colleges. Founded in 1977, the society had forty chapters across the country. Alpha Beta Kappa

Basketball at Madison Business College.

- *Bilingual Student Exchange Program
  American Business Academy of San Jose, Costa Rica, and Portsmouth Interstate Business College of Portsmouth, Ohio have initiated a bilingual secretarial exchange program.*

- *Supermarket Checker Course
  An in-service course designed to prepare teachers and industry trainers to teach a successful supermarket checker course.*

- *Help Coming for Overnight Optometrists
  One and two-year courses of study which include lectures and laboratory work supplemented by actual experience. Paraoptometrists may do laboratory work, assist with contact lens work, help with visual training, and office administration.*

—From The Compass

---

was intended for honor students; applicants came from the top 10 percent of their classes. AICS member schools with chapters included Bay State Junior College of Boston, Massachusetts; Johnson & Wales College of Providence, Rhode Island; The Katharine Gibbs School of New York, New York; Pueblo College of Business in Pueblo, Colorado; Betz College of Cincinnati, Ohio; Jefferson Business College in Washington, D.C.; and Crandall Junior College of Macon, Georgia.

COMPUTERS

Automation was a big buzz word back in the 1950s. Many people talked about automation, some knowing it would be the wave of the future, while others feared the changes. Some adopted a wait-and-see attitude toward automation. When computers finally made their way into businesses and offices across the country in the late 1970s, keyboarding, word processing, and using spreadsheets became important skills. As a result, the Association and the private career sector became closely involved with computer instruction and computer support services.

Publishers began to sense the future demand for computer instruction in the late 1960s. In 1963, McGraw-Hill Book Company published a series of five college textbooks on computer use. The texts offered a full curriculum in data processing, and the series contained all necessary materials, including teachers' manuals and other ancillaries. Other publishers joined the field in the 1970s. Advances in computer hardware and software developed rapidly, and it was difficult for new publications to keep up with the quickly changing technology.

Much was written about word processing in the early 1970s, but little was known about its possible applications. For example, an article in *The Wall Street Journal* stated that "Dividing up the secretary's world and introducing new office gadgetry are parts of a broad concept known as word processing." This definition certainly didn't clarify our vague notions about

what word processing really was or what it would become. Who would have believed, fifteen years ago, how specific and functional word processing would someday become?

In 1979 and 1980, AICS sponsored seven word-processing institutes in collaboration with Bobbs-Merrill Educational Publishing. Various cities from coast to coast were chosen as sites for the programs. The one-day workshops focused on the latest trends in the field, as well as on the functions and possible applications of word processing. These types of events indicated growing awareness that word processing had arrived as a vital discipline in the age of technology. It was not long before word processing became a popular course at many AICS member schools.

AICS Compass published several articles in the early 1980s on word processing. These were written by Delores Curley of the Detroit College of Business, and they focused on familiarizing educators and administrators with the latest applications and trends. Since each passing year brought more innovations to the word processing field, Curley was careful to keep readers informed of the latest technology and applications. Her writings reflected the inevitability that traditional office typewriters were being replaced by more advanced machines, and time has proven her correct.

Although word processing was of primary interest, other computer applications caught the attention of private career educators. As various software packages flooded the market, private career schools designed courses to teach their applications. Courses in Lotus, Symphony, and a host of other software programs have been popular at many schools. Keyboarding and general computer techniques also became important aspects of courses of study in AICS schools by 1985.

CORPORATE DIVERSIFICATION

Before the turn of the century, there were several large school chains in the private career sector. You may recall from previous chapters that two of the

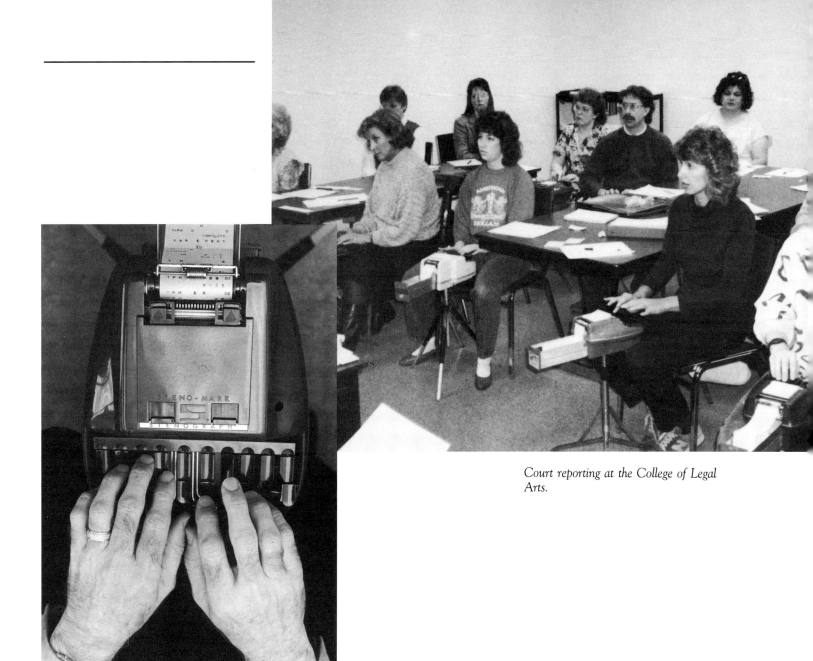

Court reporting at the College of Legal Arts.

Court stenography.

most successful chains were the Bryant and Stratton Schools and the Draughon Schools. As the twentieth century progressed, however, most of these large chains fragmented and reverted to independent ownership.

In the 1960s, a resurgence of chain schools developed, though with a slightly different approach to ownership. Many large manufacturing and service corporations decided that one form of diversification might be to acquire career schools as part of their holdings. As a result, many publicly held corporations became holding companies for business, trade, and technical schools.

The LSI Systems and Services Group, a division of the Lear Siegler Corporation, was one of the first to enter the private school field. In 1968 LSI acquired the Nettleton Colleges' business training schools in South Dakota, Nebraska, and Iowa. Lear Siegler went on to acquire schools in Louisiana, Washington, California, Oklahoma, and Ohio, bringing the number of schools to thirty with a total enrollment of 22,000 students.

International Telephone and Telegraph Company (ITT) also actively pursued diversification in the early 1960s. Along with acquiring Avis Rent-A-Car, Sheraton Hotels, Aetna Finance, and the Speedwriting Company, the firm purchased the Temple chain of schools. Temple had owned a number of schools in Virginia,

Our Graduates Get More

Than An Education

They Get Good Jobs!

Reprinted from AICS Compass.

Maryland, and the District of Columbia, and all of them became part of ITT's Educational Services.

The LTV Aerospace Corporation also became a buyer of private career schools. LTV established a special division in 1969, the LTV Education System Inc., to accommodate their school acquisitions. In 1971 LTV announced the purchase of five additional business colleges in Texas and New Mexico. With these acquisitions, LTV had acquired fifteen business and trade schools since establishing their education division. LTV hired G.C. Stewart, a longtime Association member, to serve as General Operations Manager for the College Division of LTV Education System.

Life Insurance Company of Virginia entered the private career school sector through the formation of its Bradford School Corporation. In August 1970, C. Fred Burdett, who had served as President of Burdett College in Boston for thirty-five years, announced his retirement and the sale of his ninety-year-old institution to the Bradford School Corporation. With the purchase of Burdett College, the Life Insurance Company of Virginia expanded the growing list of schools and colleges under its corporate umbrella.

Another formidable corporation entered the private school field in 1971. General Electric Company's educational affiliate, General Learning Corporation, began purchasing private career schools. CBS Schools was another division that developed in the

early 1970s and the Dictaphone Company also began acquiring schools. Thus, the educational competition between several corporate giants of the time became intensified.

Apparently, this avenue of diversification did not work well for many of the corporations. In hindsight, the private career school business was simply too specialized and too personalized for their large-scale management techniques. Little by little, they began selling their holdings, and many are now no longer associated with the private career schools at all. (Several of these corporate giants have themselves been swallowed by bigger fish in recent times.)

Some new corporate giants have entered the field over the past several years. However, most of these firms were experienced in education-related services. Two of these are the Macmillan Publishing Company and Josten's. In the late 1970s and early 1980s an interesting phenomenon began to develop. The movement was a sort of rebirth of the early school chain concept in which a successful private career school owner acquired additional schools. At present, several large holding companies of this type—devoted to private school education—exist. Some are operated as publicly held corporations, while others are privately owned.

MEMORIES

Conventions have always provided fond memories for the membership. They have served as times of renewal, fellowship, and opportunities to explore new ideas. In the early days, annual conventions were traditionally held during the last week of the calendar year. For the past several decades, however, the conventions have been held in the fall, usually in late October or early November.

The conventions have also been hosted in new cities over the past quarter century, in addition to the more traditional sites. Las Vegas was one of the more flamboyant locations. In 1970 a long but enjoyable journey was undertaken to Honolulu, Hawaii. The

Association returned to Hawaii in 1984 when it convened on the beautiful island of Maui. International sites have also been chosen. The lovely city of Montreal, Canada, was the location of the 1971 annual meeting. Bermuda welcomed AICS for its sixty-eighth annual convention, and Puerto Rico also hosted a recent convention. Association members have convened in New Orleans, San Francisco, and Washington, D.C., over the years, and they seem to enjoy returning to these cities. In fact, Washington, D.C., is where the Association is celebrating its Diamond Jubilee convention in October 1987.

Among the significant memories are the affiliations that the Association has made over the decades. The concept of allied membership within the Association really caught on after the UBSA was formed in 1962. *The Compass* listed twenty-three allied members in its January 1963 issue. These allied members included the Baxandall public relations firm; the Comptometer Corporation; the Gregg Division of McGraw-Hill Book Company; the IBM Corporation; Prentice-Hall, Inc.; the H.M. Rowe Company; Stenographic Machines; and the South-Western Publishing Co., Inc.

The UBSA was extremely supportive of other organizations that strived to improve the quality of education. For example, the UBSA generously supported the Business and Office Occupations Division of the American Vocational Association. At the AVA convention in Minneapolis in 1964, Executive Director Fulton presented a check to Elvin S. Eyster of the AVA for membership dues for about 450 UBSA administrators. In addition, UBSA members participated actively in AVA matters.

In 1974 plans were announced to approve the merger of the two national associations responsible for coordinating and monitoring accreditation of postsecondary institutions and programs. The boards of the National Commission of Accrediting, in Chicago, and the Council of the Federation of Regional Accrediting Commissions of Higher Education, in Atlanta, officially approved the merger. The new organization was named the Council on Postsecondary Accredi-

Karen Hudson, representing Phi Beta Lambda, presents a plaque to Floyd Gassaway, President of Sanford-Brown College, honoring him for his work in the career education field.

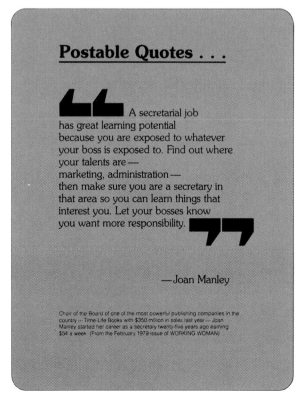

Postable Quotes . . .

" A secretarial job has great learning potential because you are exposed to whatever your boss is exposed to. Find out where your talents are — marketing, administration — then make sure you are a secretary in that area so you can learn things that interest you. Let your bosses know you want more responsibility. **"**

—Joan Manley

Chair of the Board of one of the most powerful publishing companies in the country — Time-Life Books with $350 million in sales last year — Joan Manley started her career as a secretary twenty-five years ago earning $54 a week. (From the February 1979 issue of WORKING WOMAN)

Reprinted from AICS Compass.

Franklin F. Moore Memorial Library at Rider College.

LARGEST SHORTHAND COLLECTION

In 1984, a shorthand collection containing approximately 15,000 items was bequeathed to Rider College in Lawrenceville, New Jersey. The collection includes shorthand periodicals, shorthand books in many languages, and several books inscribed by such notables as John Robert Gregg and Sir Isaac Pitman. The collection shows how authors handled copyright problems in the 18th century and includes letters written in shorthand by soldiers during the Civil War.

The items, currently being catalogued, will be housed in the Franklin F. Moore Library.

—From The Compass

tation (COPA). The AICS Accrediting Commission has been a longstanding member of COPA.

In 1981 AICS President Friedheim announced a new affiliation. AICS was accepted as a member in the American Assembly of Collegiate Schools of Business (AACSB). The Association joined the AACSB to demonstrate their common interest in students who wished to pursue a career in business, and to take part in the process of developing academic programs in business education.

Miami-Jacobs College of Dayton, Ohio, has enjoyed special attention over the years. The college was featured in the 1966 Steve Canyon syndicated comic strip, which revealed Poteet Canyon beginning her studies at Ludlow College of Business, a fictitious school modeled after Miami-Jacobs. Mr. Ludlow, the president of the college, was a thinly disguised Charles Harbottle, the real president of Miami-Jacobs. The strip's creator, Milton Caniff, was a member of the Miami-Jacobs Steering Committee for its one-hundred-twenty-fifth anniversary in 1985. A photograph of Miami-Jacobs also appeared in the January–February 1987 edition of *Change* magazine, as part of an article on private career education. The college has had a succession of presidents from the same family since 1903, when William Harbottle began his tenure as president. He served until his death in 1954. Charles Harbottle followed as president for thirty years; in 1984 he was elected as the chairman of the board of Dayton Business College. He was succeeded by his nephew, Charles G. Campbell.

Along with the fond memories, there have also been some sad moments in the history of the Association and its members. C.W. Woodward, one of the founding members of the American Association of Commercial Colleges and its executive secretary for more than thirty years, died in 1968 at the age of seventy-seven. Raymond W. Baxandall, owner of the Baxandall Company, which published advertising for many independent schools, died in 1970. Baxandall was remembered as a close friend of many AICS member institutions.

A finished food shot might look simple, but it requires considerable planning.

In 1973 Harold D. Hopkins died at the age of eighty-five. Dr. Hopkins had served as the first executive secretary of the Association, from 1951 to 1958. He also served as executive secretary of the Accrediting Commission for Business Schools from 1958 to 1962. After many years of service, he joined Fort Lauderdale University as an academic dean and professor of English, and retired as Professor Emeritus in 1970. Before joining the NACBS in 1951, Dr. Hopkins had been president of Defiance College in Ohio.

Another well-respected man in the private career sector, Dr. Jay W. Miller, died on April 11, 1975, at his winter home in Sun City, Florida. Dr. Miller was eighty-one years old at the time of his death. Miller was best remembered as a nationally recognized educator, an active Association member, and a prolific writer. He retired as president of Goldey Beacom College in 1968.

HISTORY AND HINDSIGHT

Oliver Wendell Holmes, Jr., stated it best, "When I want to understand what is happening today or try to decide what will happen tomorrow, I look back." In previous sections, we have taken a long look back at the history of AICS to gain some insights into its present and its future. Now it is time to use those insights to look ahead and see what tomorrow holds for the Association.

Brooks Institute photographers check the results of an undersea test shoot during an expedition in the Sea of Cortez.

Chapter 6

Beyond

"Hindsight is always twenty-twenty," according to a popular saying. Our vision of the future, on the other hand, is almost always myopic and, at best, slated for a low probability of accuracy. Imagine if the founders of the Association were alive today to see the progress and change that have occurred in private career education! Imagine if Fra Pacioli, the founder of the double-entry bookkeeping system, could be here to see how sophisticated and intricate the theory and practice of accounting have become. Furthermore, what would he think about the technological tools that are now used to facilitate accounting practices? What would Edward F. Underhill, the author of the first typewriting manual, write about the complex computers and word processors that are currently replacing typewriters? Imagine how surprised the early vocational educators would be at the new subjects taught in AICS institutions today, such as electronics, health care, fashion, and computers.

Up to this point, we have positioned our telescopes to look back as far as 1494. Now we turn them 180 degrees to look into the future years of the Association. We'll concentrate our efforts from the present to 2012, the year in which AICS will celebrate its one-hundredth birthday.

The history of the last seventy-five years has taught us a lesson or two. We know for certain that the next twenty-five years will be years of exciting and continuous change for private career education. In addition, we know that to meet the demands of the times we must remain in the forefront of educational innovation. Regardless of the many changes to come, the basic mission of "learning to earn" will alway prevail in the private school sector.

THE ECONOMIC FORECAST

While it is difficult enough to get economists to agree on the causes and effects of historical events, it is even more difficult to get them to concur on what will happen next month or next year. To find consensus among economists about where the American economy will be fifteen or twenty-

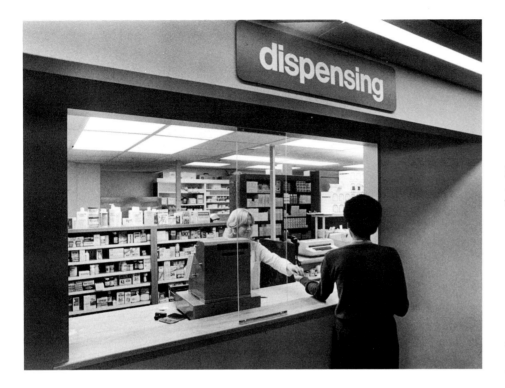

It is expected that many new jobs in the 1990s will be filled by women and minorities.

five years down the road is virtually impossible. However, recent forecasts by reliable research agencies have shed light on what the economy will look like in the 1990s. We will use these forecasts to set the stage for predictions related to the private career school sector.

Estimates indicate that between 1987 and the year 2000 there will be 18 million new jobs created in this nation's economy. Nine out of ten of these new jobs will be in the service industries. Eight out of ten of these new jobs will be filled by women, minorities, and immigrants. About 3.5 million of these new jobs will be part-time positions. Most of these are also expected to be filled by women, some of whom will divide their time between working at home and working at paid jobs. In addition, semiretired, older people will fill an increasing proportion of the new part-time positions both to supplement meager retirement funds and to remain active and useful as they grow older.

Some forecasters believe that the middle class will prosper during the next few decades; others predict that it will not. Those that favor prosperity base their predictions on the fact that the baby boom population has hit middle age and that the generations that followed have been much smaller. This means that there will be fewer workers to fill more jobs in the future. The "baby bust" of the 1960s closed many classrooms in the public schools

during the 1970s. By 1995, the number of teenagers entering the work force will be about 27 percent below the 1978 peak. As a result, the entry-level positions will be harder for employers to fill; therefore, entry-level wages will be much higher. Employers are already beginning to feel the effects of the early stages of this demographic reality.

United States production of automobiles and steel is not expected to diminish further in the years ahead. While these industries may not grow, their recent gradual declines are not expected to continue. In the manufacturing sector, high-tech industries will prevail. Computers, robotics, scientific products, pharmacology, and communications are examples of key growth industries for the future. Competition, both domestic and foreign, will be fierce. As a result, change will become a constant, and American workers will become accustomed to training for two or three careers during their working lives. Education will need to serve both those students who are being prepared for their first careers and those who are returning to school to learn new job skills. The private career institutions will continue to train and retrain.

Despite the tremendous growth of the service sector in our economy over the past fifteen years, there has been little research conducted in management techniques for service industries. Most analysts agree that pro-

Growth trends in electronics, computers, and other high-tech industries are expected to continue.

Processing of information is critical to what is taught now and in the future.

ductivity growth in the service field lags far behind that in the manufacturing area. Lack of academic training and expertise on the job could become a problem as the service sector continues to expand. This could be particularly critical when one considers that probably more than two-thirds of the United States economy will be engaged in the service sector by the year 2000.

The average family size is expected to remain small; therefore, population growth is projected to be slow in the next few decades. The Hispanic and black populations are growing more rapidly than the white population. These groups will eventually make up a greater proportion of the United States population. And, if current growth trends continue, Hispanics will displace blacks as the largest minority group in the United States by the turn of the century.

THE INFORMATION AGE

As part of its 1986 Annual Report, Bell South Corporation invited five creative thinkers to share their views on the future, particularly in terms of the information age. Since information and communications are so critical to what we now teach and to what we will continue to teach in the future, it might be enlightening to share some of the predictions of this distinguished group.

Among those diverse experts offering their opinions in the report was Professor Martin Feldstein, an economics faculty member of Harvard University, and a former chairman of the White House Council of Economic Advisers. Feldstein forecasts a relatively quick end to the depressed state of the industrial sector of the American economy. He sees a resurgence of manufacturing and the development of new world markets for American goods over the next decade.

Another of the panelists, Catherine Ross, an associate professor of City Planning at the Georgia Institute of Technology and a recognized authority on transportation, provides an optimistic view of the information age. She believes that one result of the current telecommunications surge in the workplace, a growth that should continue for some time, is that people will have more time for leisure activities.

James Dickey, author of *Deliverance*, and the recipient of numerous literary honors, was another of the Bell South commentators. Dickey notes that wherever the future takes us, we can always carry along our literary past in both the electronic and print forms.

Dr. Terrel Bell, a professor of educational administration at the University of Utah and former United States Secretary of Education, believes that education holds the key to the future of the economy:

Anyone concerned with the future of the United States has to care about education. We can no longer get by on the richness of our natural resources alone. Our prime resource is human intelligence, and if we don't cultivate it, I believe we're going to become an economic colony of the Pacific Rim.

We compete in a global marketplace. We have to learn to be excellent, to perform at the outer layer of our ability. The place to learn that is in school, in an educational system that inspires students to develop their talents.

Alvin Toffler, another contributor to the Bell South report, who is well known for his many commentaries about the future, concludes that the rapid growth in electronic information will eventually allow people more freedom in their daily lives:

Millions of words have been written about the communications revolution, but little has been said about why it's happening now. As the Industrial Age developed a more complex division of labor, the channels of communication became overloaded. With goods produced in one place and consumed elsewhere, it became necessary to exchange more information. New technologies—from the post office to the steam-driven printing press—arose to make that possible. . . .

But the information we now get gives us only fragmentary pictures of the world. Synthesis of these fragments is the major intellectual and managerial task of our time. My dream newspaper of the future would not carry 'only the news I need to know.' It would have ten stories on page one and one story showing how the ten connect.

This tourism and hotel class at Cannon's International Business College reflects the growing interest in leisure time management.

Communication is becoming more asynchronous. Videocassettes permit us to watch a movie when we want to see it instead of at an hour set by the network. Computers let me send my messages now and let you receive it when you want. The pulsing mass rhythm of industrial society in which everyone's day follows a similar schedule is giving way to highly personalized rhythms.

THANKS TO THE SOOTHSAYERS

Predicting what is ahead for the Association of Independent Colleges and Schools and its member schools is an overwhelming challenge. To paint a comprehensive portrait of what the Association is likely to look like twenty-five years from now, Association President Jerry Miller invited the advisory committee of the seventy-fifth anniversary book to help forecast AICS's future. The Association's staff formulated and mailed a three-page survey to the twenty-five members of the advisory committee. These people, all prominent private career school administrators, educators, or associates, were asked to complete the questionnaire or to engage others with expertise to do so on their behalf.

The response to this survey request was outstanding. Several committee members included additional information, and many requested colleagues in their schools to provide them with additional input, creating a more diverse range of opinions. A few advisory members responded by summarizing events of the past as a basis for predicting the future. In addition to these surveys, we also used the transcribed presentations of Jack Yena and Jan Friedheim, both of whom spoke about the future of private career schools at the 1986 AICS convention in Colorado Springs.

Sincere appreciation is extended to this panel of crystal-ball gazers. Without their help, most of the forecasts that follow would not have been possible. Perhaps twenty-five years from now they will receive the praise they deserve for their predictive talents.

Traditional courses, such as accounting and typing, remain the core of private career education.

WHO WILL WE TEACH IN THE FUTURE?

The members of the advisory committee reached an amazing degree of consensus on the question of who we will teach in AICS institutions in the future. Most of them agreed that there will continue to be a market for the traditional private career school student well beyond the year 2000. The traditional students are those young adults with postsecondary credentials who wish to obtain a certificate, diploma, or degree in a specialized area of career education. Many of these students are dropouts from four-year programs, who decide, after a year or two, to go back to school to learn a skill or acquire a degree in a specific career area.

In addition, a major new market of students, made up of adults in need of retraining, will develop over the next twenty-five years. These adults will be primarily between the ages of 35 and 65 and will be seeking new skills in order to keep up with the job market. Some will be displaced workers from the "Rust Belt," whose manufacturing jobs in industries such as steel and automobiles have been eliminated or replaced by automation. Others, who have retired from one job, will be seeking new skills in order to work part-time in a new career. The part-time job market will also employ many single parents, a large proportion of whom will be black or Hispanic. This employment pattern will be most visible in large urban areas.

Many of our crystal-ball gazers see competition from the public sector for career students becoming more intense in the decades ahead. This is because increased pressure will be placed on public institutions to find the enrollments to justify their budget appropriations. As a result, private career schools will need to offer more courses in the evening and on weekends. This will help in the competitive battle to accommodate students who have work or home commitments during the day. This pattern of part-time evening instruction is very similar to the night schools and evening college classes that served so many

Culinary studies were added to curricula to fill the need for highly trained food personnel in resort areas.

145

As the use of high-tech equipment increases in foreign countries, students in these countries will seek specialized technical training.

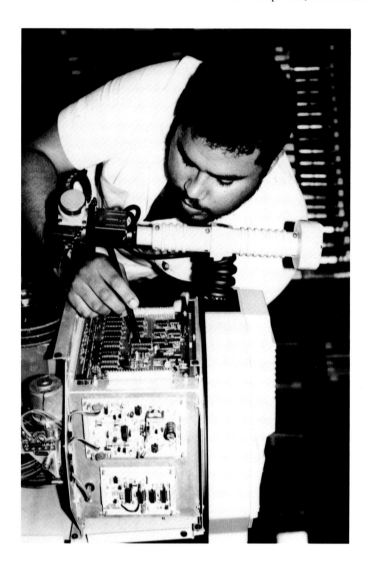

working students and veterans after World War II.

Several of our forecasters see "contract learning" as becoming a vital part of services offered by member schools in the future. Contract learning involves providing specific programs of study or training for certain employers and their employees, either on their premises or at a contracted school. Many contend that businesses and government agencies are beginning to realize that contract learning is a less expensive and more productive way to train employees, and that AICS member schools have considerable expertise in this area of education.

Some of our respondents believe that foreign students coming to the United States for an education will choose private career schools much more frequently in the future. As the use of computers and other high-tech devices increases in foreign countries, students from those countries will want to work in related occupations. Consequently, they will seek training that will prepare them as quickly and efficiently as possible for specialized technical vocations. They will come to the United States because America's reputation for providing this kind of high-quality career education is already well established.

One of our prognosticators, with many years of experience in private career education, made the following observation: "We have gone from educating the pre-World War II farmer and white high school graduate to primarily educating the veterans after the war. During the late '60s, and through the '70s and '80s, we have concentrated much of our efforts on helping to train the disadvantaged. The future for the private school will be in education for second career people."

All of our futurists are optimistic about the continued growth and development of the private career sector. However, most caution that the private career schools must remain flexible, distinctive and personalized, and ready to change with the demands of the times.

WHAT WILL WE TEACH?

French poet Paul Ambroise Valery made this very apropos observation about futurism: "The trouble with our times is that the future is not what it used to be." This wry comment is applicable to our dilemma of trying to determine what we will be teaching in the future. Because needs will arise to teach many subjects that do not even exist at present, it is hard to envision all of the areas of study we will be offering twenty-five years from now. Who could have predicted twenty-five years ago the wonders of CAT scan technology or the spectacular development of computer technology? Thus, no matter what we project as the future subjects, we are destined to be guilty of some significant omissions.

The advisory committee members who responded to the survey agree that accounting and secretarial subjects, as well as management, health care, and paraprofessional areas, will all continue to be major programs for career schools. However, they see significant changes in the course content in each of these programs. For example, the secretarial programs will no longer emphasize shorthand and typewriting to the extent that they do today. Word processing, keyboarding, communications, and printing technology will be stressed instead. Secretaries will have to remain skillful in human relations but also become more adept as technicians.

Paraprofessional programs in medicine, law, accounting, and teaching should increase in AICS member in-

Paraprofessional programs in law, medicine, accounting, and teaching are expected to increase in AICS institutions.

stitutions of the future. Doctors, lawyers, and other professionals find themselves offering more and more technology-related services to their patients and clients. When paraprofessionals assist with or perform these services, the doctors or lawyers can spend their time on more creative tasks. In addition, using paraprofessionals to provide technical services can reduce the costs of those services to patients and clients. Private career schools can take the lead in providing paraprofessional training in the future. Many are already in the forefront in this area of training today.

Some forecasters see the private career school engaging extensively in programs related to leisure-life services. They point to the increasing demand for courses of study in travel, recreation management, arts and entertainment administration, sports administration, nutrition, and physical-fitness management. They also indicate the need for additional high-quality food service programs, as well as courses of study in hotel operations, customer relations, security, and law enforcement.

Computer education will continue to be a focal point in the future. Traditional computer orientation courses

Programs in hospital care and home health services are being added to the curriculum at AICS institutions.

will gradually be replaced by more specialized courses as the population attains a greater degree of computer literacy. Computer-aided design (CAD), the computer application of many of the tasks of interior designers, is one such area of specialized training that is now being taught in some AICS schools. Other major areas of computer training that will grow in the future include communications and networking as well as computer servicing and repair. Of course, word processing, data entry, computer-assisted accounting, management support systems, and file set-up and retrieval will become more dominant in the curriculum than they are today.

Basic skills will still be required in the future, and some of our predictors believe the opportunities to teach these will increase. They reason that no matter how advanced the technology, people will still need to know how to read, write, and communicate. They will also need to understand basic functions of mathematics and to be adept at using the English language. For these reasons, many adults seeking a second career, and many foreign-born citizens and foreigners, will need to learn basic skills. In addition, the GED (Graduate Equivalency Diploma) will become a necessary alternative for the increasing number of people who do not complete high school. This presents another opportunity for private career schools: to engage in nondegree remediation programs.

The advisory committee also predicts growth in programs for careers in real estate and insurance, and training for managerial and paraprofessional positions in financial securities services. There may also be a need to train teachers for corporate classrooms as well as educational institutions. In addition, home health and hospital care services are two other important disciplines that should continue to grow in private career schools.

Here are some general comments indicating how some of the respondents to our survey see the role of private career colleges in the future.

Said one respondent: "Our schools will continue to offer a basic business curriculum. In fact, the new statistics show that four out of five entering freshmen choose a business major. A second area of growth for private schools will be training programs in paraprofessional areas. Because of our cost-conscious society, the need for paraprofessionals such as paralegals, medical assistants, and library assistants will increase."

Another said that "We will continue to teach business and technical courses. Our schools will begin to realize the importance of communication skills. We will teach more recreation or pleasure type courses to senior citizens and nonworking spouses. We may attempt to teach more social skills along with whatever high-tech careers become popular in the future."

Another's view was that "While word processing skills might replace typewriting skills; while computer operational skills might replace 10-key adding machine skills; and while using a computer spelling bank might replace use of the dictionary in instruction, the fundamental teaching of manipulative skills, English, writing, and communication will continue to prevail and predominate."

A final word: "We will continue to emphasize communications to supplement and improve the basic education and training level offered in the high schools and junior colleges. Computer programming will continue strong for a while until developments in software are made to eliminate the complications and difficulties that now require specialized training in order to tell even a minicomputer what to do. I believe our courses will be enriched by greater emphasis on merchandising, marketing, and various services."

WHO WILL PAY TUITION COSTS?

Generally, the members of the advisory committee agreed that government, on both the state and federal levels, will continue to provide grants to students and subsidize tuition loans. However, in the short run, the amount of money available in these funds will not increase significantly over present levels. A few believe that as the pendulum swings there will be a return to

Mass media students at Central Pennsylvania Business School train in a fully equipped video studio on campus.

significant increases in federal and state funding in the late 1990s.

Most of our prophets believe that federal and state government will continue to provide funding to the private career schools. They think that lawmakers are convinced that private career education is not an expense of government but instead an investment in the future of this country. Therefore, the urban poor will continue to receive public assistance tuition allocations. One problem, however, is that the sentiments of lawmakers are not the same toward those in the low-middle- to middle-income brackets. Federal and state funds for students coming from families in this income range have dropped off considerably and most likely will continue to do so for several more years.

If tuition costs climb and government assistance remains static, or even declines, there will be a financial gap that many students will find difficult to fill. Many of our prognosticators believe that students, especially those in the middle-income sector, will have to pay out of pocket and borrow to meet financial needs in the private

Laboratory technology students get hands-on experience in fully equipped laboratories.

Financial aid is a constantly changing, complicated field. Financial aid officers must keep abreast of the current regulatory issues that affect student aid. They must be able to review and interpret correctly new regulations and keep up-to-date on the changes in the various campus-based programs. This conference will offer regulatory up-dates and interpretations, and will be modified up to the very last possible moment in order to offer the very latest in regulatory changes from the Department of Education.

—From AICS 1987 Advanced Financial Aid Conference brochure

sector. One alternative may be to pool the resources of private career schools and their educators to provide low-interest loans to students. Another possibility would be to inform consumers of the advantages of establishing a tuition annuity similar to an insurance annuity. Under such a plan, a parent would open a regular savings program when a child is very young, and the savings, together with its compounded interest, would provide the necessary tuition funds for the student to enter the private career school.

Some forecasters believe that in the future specific federal and state government agencies will provide grants and loans for students who qualify as members of small, narrowly defined groups. They believe these funds will replace the grants and loans that now come out of the general treasury and are available to students in much broader population groups. For example, the Veterans Administration would provide funds to veterans, state agencies that serve the deaf and blind would provide funding for students in those categories, and the Bureau of Indian Affairs would subsidize Native

American students. In the future, deficit-plagued federal and state legislatures may be more willing to support these kinds of specialized grants than to support broader and more-expensive aid programs.

Several members of the advisory committee contend that as contract education becomes more prevalent in the private career sector, increasing numbers of employers will pay the costs of specialized training. Furthermore, as employers become more confident about the quality of the services provided by career schools, they will fund endowments and special scholarship programs. In some cases, all of the companies engaged in a particular industry may combine their resources to offer low-interest loans, grants, and scholarships to workers who desire to go back to school and retrain themselves for a new career within the industry.

One of our soothsayers presented this interesting viewpoint on future tuition costs:

Twenty-five years ago tuition and other costs were the responsibility of the student and parents. Today there has been a shift to state and federal assistance in paying college costs. Most activities here in the United States seem to be on a credit basis. That will expand tremendously in the next twenty-five years. It would appear to me that education will become almost totally subsidized through loans or a line of credit, perhaps as much as $60,000 to $100,000 to pay for one's education, with a long-term payback much the same as one would pay for a house. A thorough education during the next twenty-five years may have more meaning than a house does today. This will be primarily because people will be far more mobile, and they will need skills to survive in a very competitive environment. There may be some in the future who pay cash for education, but the state and federal government will continue to play a very important role in financing education, or at least in guaranteeing loans from financial institutions.

The average tuition for a good business school in 1921 was $48 a quarter (three months). In 1963, the average tuition was $230 a quarter and by 1987, it had risen to $1,500 a quarter. Tuition has increased almost seven times during the last twenty-five years. During the next quarter century, average tuition could possibly go up to $10,000 a quarter, or $30,000 a year. It

Students design and print advertisements, tickets, and programs for clubs and class activities.

will probably continue to take the joint effort of the student, the state, and the federal government to finance one's tuition.

SIZE AND STRUCTURE OF MEMBER SCHOOLS

Will the number of AICS schools and the student population grow, remain the same, or decrease over the next twenty-five years? What will the organizational structure of these schools be in terms of ownership and management? The answers we received to these questions were quite varied, though somewhat limited in scope. Apparently the advisory committee members found the crystal ball a bit clouded when they tried to visualize our future size and structure.

Most of our soothsayers believe that the number of Association member schools will remain at about the present level, or perhaps even drop slightly. However, in terms of size, they predict that on the average there will be more full-time students in each school. Most estimates for the average full-time student body were around 500. Since each school will have more students on the average, it is anticipated that each school will offer more programs. This is consistent with current practices in AICS member institutions where even schools with large enrollments strive to offer individualized instruction in small-sized classes.

Most of the members of the advisory committee believe that the major growth in numbers of students is likely

Students enjoy a few quiet moments in their busy schedules.

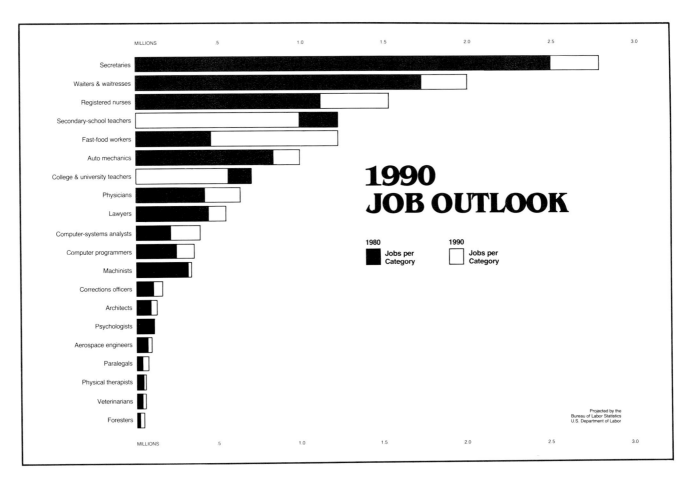

1990 JOB OUTLOOK

1980 ■ Jobs per Category

1990 □ Jobs per Category

Projected by the
Bureau of Labor Statistics
U.S. Department of Labor

to take place in business-related programs. Many predicted a 15 to 20 percent increase in student population by 2012. This amounts to less than a 1 percent annual increase and lags behind increases predicted in the United States population, the gross national product, and United States annual productivity rates for the same period. On the other hand, one of our stargazers believes that student population will triple over current levels during the next quarter century! (We are all hoping that he is right!)

The advisory committee members hold a much greater diversity of opinions over the question of how schools will be structured and managed in the future than they do over the question of growth. Some believe that more schools will operate under the structure of an umbrella arrangement, and that corporate chain ownership, a current trend of some proportion, will continue through the 1990s. Others take the completely opposite point of view. They believe that the days of growing school chains are coming to an end. These futurists foresee a return to locally owned schools operated

by people who come from the community. A few even predict a return to the "mom and pop" schools that were so prevalent in the early days of the Association. In summary, our forecasters see opportunities for various kinds of ownership structures in the years ahead. (This is consistent with the history of private career education over the past 150 years.)

Many expect the phenomenon in education known as "schools without walls" to become a force in the private career sector. They predict this increase in off-site training will take place as a result of the higher demand for contract education. Many of the school's educational services will be provided on the premises of the employers who engage them. They see the same off-site instruction taking place in locations such as shopping centers and government buildings because government agencies will want some of the training that they fund to take place in areas easily accessible to large numbers of their clients and employees.

Jack Yena, speaking at the 1986 AICS convention in Colorado Springs, addressed the size and structure issue as follows: "We will probably have two kinds of shapes in the future. One will be the smaller schools serving local populations, remaining flexible to their needs, as were many of the early schools. The second will be a few larger schools—strong institutions—with unlimited resources. There will be a demise of all the schools in between who do not have a set purpose or reason for being."

FUTURE LEARNING RESOURCES

What resources will be needed to provide the highest-quality education to students in the future? The committee members agree that the most important resource will continue to be the teacher. They feel that the person-to-person interaction between teachers and students that private career schools currently provide is an essential factor in providing high-quality education, and that it will remain a critical element in the future.

Instructors in the future will need to develop different teaching methods to accommodate new technologies and environmental changes if they are to remain competitive. While the teacher will continue to be at the center of the instructional process, technology will play an important role in enhancing and reinforcing what is taught in the classroom. Teachers will need to be experts on how, why, and when it is most appropriate to use computers, television, and telecommunications as instructional aids. They will need to stay current in their subjects and with the latest teaching methods and classroom management techniques. This new partnership of teacher and technology will also make it very easy to diagnose the needs of each student and to design individualized learning programs for them. It should be emphasized that this partnership will not be an equal one. The teacher will be the controlling partner.

Future administrators will be required to spend more time and effort learning about this new partnership between teacher and technology. Ad-

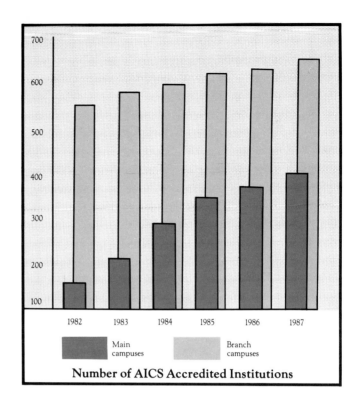

Number of AICS Accredited Institutions

Main campuses

Branch campuses

A Growing Success Story

A study commissioned by AICS and conducted by Dr. Carol Frances, chief economic advisor for Washington Resources, Inc., shows that membership in the Association has increased by 13 percent over the last two years and that enrollment in AICS institutions has increased by approximately 50,000 students each year for the past six years. According to the study, when viewed in terms of the number of students served each year and the expanding facilities, private career schools and colleges are clearly the fastest growing sector of post-secondary education.

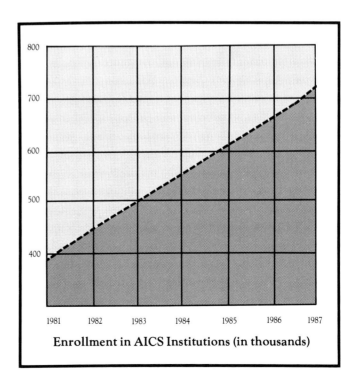

Enrollment in AICS Institutions (in thousands)

Nine out of ten jobs in the 1990s will be in service industries.

cal devices should be utilized by the teacher. Employers will also be called on more frequently to serve as guest teachers, especially in·courses of a high-tech nature. In addition to employers, other organizations, such as chambers of commerce, government agencies, trade associations, and economic development councils, will need to be involved in private career education in similar ways. Finally, AICS will be expected to provide more seminars and workshops focusing on the teacher/technology partnership and the administrative requirements for managing that partnership.

Some predict that it will be necessary for consortiums to be established for member schools so that they may share knowledge, equipment, and techniques to provide increased instructional productivity at a low cost. In addition, students at all member schools will be required to take competency tests both when they enter and complete courses so that the schools can gather broad statistics to measure learning progress and to monitor the efficiency of the new teaching technology.

The costs of the new learning partnership between teachers and technology will be high, but it is hoped that a combination of factors will help relieve this burden. One such factor might be the sharing of costs through consortium arrangements among institutions. Another might be the possibility of leasing on-line learning services. A third factor is the anticipation of a natural decline in the costs of various types of high-tech equipment as their use becomes more widespread and they are mass produced.

One of our prognosticators summed up the question of future learning resources quite succinctly: "My firm opinion is that education is still basically a person-to-person enterprise. Accordingly, we must continue in the future, as in the past, to search out, train, update, assist, and keep teachers who really care about teaching as a calling—not just as a living. These [teachers] in the past few years have been harder and harder to find. In addition, however, I expect that these teachers will be assisted by more technology in doing their jobs—computer-assisted instruction, etc."

ministrators will still need to hire qualified teachers, purchase complicated technological equipment to accommodate the teaching program, and create the budgets to allocate these costs. The challenges of administration of private career education will become more complex as we move toward the next century.

Employers and business executives will be extremely important resources for private career schools in the future. Informally, they will work more closely with school administrators, providing advice and guidance, especially during the job-placement process. In a more formal manner, they will sit on advisory councils formed by the various Association member schools. (Many of these councils are already in place.) In the past, employers filled a critical need by guiding member schools in the development of new courses and changes needed in curricula. They will continue in that role in the future, but they will also provide important information about what specific training should be stressed within certain technologically oriented courses and which technologi-

HOW WILL THE ASSOCIATION CONTINUE TO SERVE MEMBERS?

What will AICS have to do differently, or what must it do in the future that it does not do now to help member schools survive and prosper for another twenty-five years? This is a tough topic, which is further complicated by its broad nature. Perhaps the ultimate answer to the question can be summarized in one word: *flexibility.*

Despite the difficulty in answering such a broad question, our soothsayers were not at a loss for solutions. Many of them believe that the accreditation function is of the greatest importance for the future growth and recognition of private career education. They believe that the Association will continue to refine its quality-control measures through the accreditation process in the future, both to overcome increased competition from public sector schools and to withstand intense public scrutiny. One direct benefit will be an informed public responding vigorously to the opportunities offered by AICS member schools and colleges.

The Association must continue to inform members of Congress and state legislators of the vital role of private career schools in the areas of postsecondary education and in the nation's economy. The most important way in which this will be done is through the Association of Independent Colleges and Schools Political Action Committee (AICSPAC), supporting and electing public officials who favor progressive education measures. Further, some advisory committee members believe that the services of AICSPAC may extend in the future to some local governments as well, particularly where those governments serve major urban areas with large ethnic groups. With regard to public information services, the advisory committee feels the AICS should continue its aggressive program to inform the general public of the role of private schools in the American system of education and of the contributions that their graduates make to society.

Sharing was a word the advisory committee members used frequently

AICS institutions respond to needs in the growing food and beverage industry.

when they discussed the question of the Association's role in the future. They see the need for the Association to provide conduits, such as on-line databases, by which member schools may share management-related statistics on enrollments, demographic trends, economic influences, marketing research, and other types of pertinent information. They also envision AICS providing a central on-line data bank to supplement individual school library resources. Students can access library resources from terminals in their own schools and receive data on-screen and through printouts. In effect, the Association would become the operator of a number of on-line database programs that could be accessed by member schools. Future needs will also require the Association to develop specific software programs for educational applications and management practices. (Some of these types of materials are already being utilized.) They also see the Association offering audiovisual packages prepared especially for students on subjects related to private career learning.

As the old joke goes: At a bacon and egg breakfast, the chicken is involved but the pig is committed! The

AICS institutions expand facilities to fill the demand for courses in the paramedical field.

advisory committee sees AICS as currently "involved" in providing its many services to its members, but in the future, the Association will become "committed" to serving member schools in a number of ways.

One way that the Association will become more committed to its members in the future is by continually exploring and devising new ways to provide financial aid to students. We discussed many possibilities in the section entitled "Who Will Pay Tuition Costs?," and the Association will be on the lookout for any other promising developments that can relieve the financial burden of career students and their parents. Also, in the future, the Association will need to provide more assistance to its member schools in disseminating financial aid information to students.

Another way in which the advisory committee believes that AICS will change in the future is that it will develop closer ties with noneducational associations, just as it has with those in the education sector. Such associations include the United States Chamber of Commerce, The American Bankers Association, and the National Association of Manufacturers. Also cited was the need for the Association to strengthen its pro-

grams in the areas of student retention and job placement.

The committee members firmly believe that the greatest opportunity for the private career sector is still ahead. If AICS plans strategically and realistically for the long term, and remains flexible, it will lead the way.

Here are some additional reflections from our advisory committee members:

The words *information explosion* will be an understatement. The future will be very exciting and profitable in meeting the educational need for the space age. To attend an AICS convention, we may ride a rocket from New York to Los Angeles and arrive in minutes. . . . Communication will play a vital role for AICS as the organization expands. There will be on-line computer access to all member schools. There will also be provisions for direct audiovisual presentations to the schools. AICS will probably depend on the large corporations for better training of management personnel, staff, and faculty to achieve a more cohesive organization. AICS will need to move into national advertising with a service program on the order of national franchising to provide appropriate membership services.

Another's view:

The number one priority must be to continue to strengthen and upgrade the accrediting process to the end that those who are accredited are models of excellence. It will also be important for the Association to deliver management assistance and training to those who, I believe, will be coming into the field as new managers or who will be establishing new local entities. I also believe that AICS should continue to develop educational testing devices, etc., in the directions now being undertaken. Finally, AICS must continue to maintain federal, and probably to some extent, state liaison, with the political bodies and regulatory bodies to insure that AICS schools continue to be recognized as valuable contributors to the nation's educational needs.

Another respondent, commenting on our need for future services, wrote that AICS will need to concentrate on "both convention offerings and seminars, plus printed materials on ways to become more efficient; how to generate better teaching; capturing and disseminating workable ideas; provision of educational networking services; provision of specialized databases applicable to our various specialties."

And finally one committee member wrote that AICS would need to offer more marketing information. "Schools are unaware of the numbers of people coming out of the high schools; dropouts from high schools; industry training and retraining programs; the adult population and their needs. . . . I believe there will be more liaison between industry, government, and private businesses to meet these needs. . . . I believe that efforts must be made to get all educational facilities recognized in every state as part of the educational picture of that state, and that efforts are made to eliminate discrimination against students so that business school students may be able to participate in all state programs."

TODAY'S INSIGHTS INTO TOMORROW

Space does not permit a discussion of all of the ideas that came forth from our survey. In tone, however, the overwhelming majority of the committee members' observations were optimistic and dynamic. Some comments were also critical or faultfinding, and we needed to hear those remarks as well if we hope to remain strong and flexible.

Many of our futurists strongly believe that private schools will have a tremendous market but that they will require effective organization, large capital outlays, proper positioning, and quality programs to cultivate it. The advisory committee members emphasized that AICS member schools must focus on continuing to meet student needs so that they can maintain their fine reputations among the learn-to-earn population of students. If we continue to concentrate on job placement for those who complete a program of study, the schools will always be successful.

Jan Friedheim, speaking at the AICS convention in Colorado Springs in October 1986, touched on the issue of change when she stated that the

Bookkeeping

Traditional courses will continue to be taught.

Secretarial science

Association must remain flexible and responsive and resist becoming too traditional. Private career schools must be open to all possibilities, such as teaching specialized courses that high schools and community colleges are not equipped to teach. This receptivity to new ideas and methods becomes more vital as manufacturing jobs are filled by robots and as employees seek retraining.

Some other notable insights from predictors follow:

- "Our future is as bright as our vision will allow. We have all the assets to make our schools successful. The only thing to fear is our own failure. We need to be able to adapt rapidly to changes in the marketplace, for whatever the student market needs, our success will depend upon our adaptability."

- "I strongly believe that those schools that succeed will be the ones who demonstrate caring attitudes toward their students. The caring attitude may be generated altruistically or through insight into what works in private proprietary education. . . . If the caring attitude doesn't exist, the private school is doomed."

- "I personally have the belief that the entrepreneurial nature of this industry will keep providing bright, creative individuals through a kind of Darwinian process. I have two beliefs about the outcome of that process: 1. That the most creative will continue to originate or to adapt ideas for new educational offerings, or offerings that will appeal to new prospect groups. . . . 2. That there will continue to be a free dissemination of ideas that work, just as has been true in the past. Through the years, particularly at the conventions, there has

been a truly selfless sharing of information. Much of it has been of the nature that it saved much research and experimentation time. Much consisted of new ideas that most of us had never before had or been exposed to."

- "I believe that our future continues to look bright provided we continue to strive for excellence in the services we deliver and the ethical manner in which we deliver them. I have never known our outlook to be otherwise—although some times have been better than others. We must protect our entrepreneur's flexibility to innovate while being certain that our most precious resource—our students—is not damaged in the process."

- "We are higher education's best kept secret. Media seems to give a hundred times more space and time to sports programs than to academics. But how can we change the general public's interests and priorities? I wish I knew."

PARTING WORDS

We have looked back to the origins of our discipline, the founders of our schools, and the development of our Association. We have reviewed the current structure and activities of the AICS and have tried to forecast the future for the private career sector and for the Association. The future is not yet clear in our sights, but it is a challenge we eagerly accept.

In October 1987, Washington, D.C., once again welcomes the AICS members, this time to the J.W. Marriott and Willard Hotels, to celebrate its Diamond Jubilee and more than 150 years of private career education in the United States. This book has been an exercise in introspection, the results of which have been extremely rewarding personally. It is sincerely hoped that the words on these pages will inspire the Association of Independent Colleges and Schools to move forward with continued pride and confidence—representing member institutions, the private career sector, and higher education—in service to America.

This is AICS—the Association, the schools, and the students.

Appendix A: 75th Anniversary Advisory Committee

Leo C. Blackburn
Chairman
Julia Corporation

Prentiss Carnell, III
President
Albany Business College

Charles W. Davidson
Chairman of the Board
Draughons College Inc.

Douglas Devaux
Chairman of the Board
Summit System of Colleges and
  Schools

James Dietz
President
Heald College

Maurice F. Egan
President Emeritus
Coleman College

Bernard H. Ehrlich
Attorney and Counselor at Law

Keith Fenton
President
American Institute of Business

Morris J. W. Gaebe
President
Johnson & Wales College

Minnie L. Gaston
President
Booker T. Washington Junior College
  of Business

Charles P. Harbottle
Chairman of the Board
Miami-Jacobs Junior College of
  Business

John W. Hauer
President
National College

Jack H. Jones
Chairman of the Board
Jones College

Howard Leffel
Former President
Kinman Business University

Larry L. Luing
President
The Berkeley Schools

Charles E. Palmer
Chairman of the Board
Strayer College, Inc.

A. Lauren Rhude
President
Chaparral Career College

Ernest E. Roblee
Former President
Jamestown Business College

Stuart E. Sears
President
Madison Business College

Robert W. Sneden
Chairman of the Board
Detroit College of Business

John T. South, Jr.
President
Cecils Junior College of Business

Weldon L. Strawn
Former President
Massey Colleges

A. R. Sullivan
President
Education Unlimited, Inc.

Walter J. Tribbey
President
Educational Management Services,
  Inc.

Mary B. Wine
Director of Professional Relations
Association of Independent Colleges
  and Schools

Appendix B: Excerpts from the 75th Anniversary Address

In 1912 a handful of our AICS predecessors joined together and committed themselves to the cooperative and creative effort that has blossomed into the complex organization we celebrate today. That was a lifetime ago!

In so many ways it was a different world. The telephone, the automobile, the electric light bulb and indoor plumbing were just catching on; talking moving pictures, commercial airplanes, television, and the computer were yet to come. Change would, however, go far deeper than technology as the very face of the world would be re-drawn in the aftermath of two world wars. . . .

Our history, as recounted in this book, in the AICS convention exhibits, and in the living stories of our individual institutions, reveals who and what we are. We look to it, neither to glorify our past nor to congratulate ourselves on how far we've come, but rather we look back for a sign of what we may become. It's an expensive and exhausting exercise. In my own view, our seventy-fifth birthday celebration could not have come at a better time. AICS needs to look at itself and to provide models for self-examination to our member colleges and schools so that they too can rediscover the already-existing sources of their future strength and growth. . . .

The personal exploration into our roots that I have undertaken during this past year as your Chairman-elect has prompted the coining of a new name for us, "Edupreneurs," to acknowledge that we have become and are a new and different breed. Today's offspring of the union of career education and entrepreneurship, which occurred in America when career education was formalized more than one hundred fifty years ago, are neither pure-bred educators nor unadulterated entrepreneurs, but a hardy hybrid species combining the most productive qualities of both their ancestors. I emphasize this point because I think it is very important, as we set our agenda for the years ahead, that we remember where we came from, who we are and what we represent.

The demographers, the economists, and the political theorists have been telling us that the world of the 1990s will be different, filled with new business opportunities accompanied by the problems inherent in every new endeavor.

We have been told for several years that the demographic sky is falling: The teenage population that fills postsecondary classrooms is declining and will be five million smaller by the early 1990s. . . . In 1983, 76% of AICS students were from families with incomes below $12,000; 53% were 22 years or older. Because we have reached out to the future and have been eager to serve both the "old" and the "new" student populations, we have been the fastest growing sector of postsecondary education during the past decade. Inherent in this tremendous growth, however, were the interrelated problems we are struggling with today, dropouts and defaults. Because we are who we are, because of our past and present, we edupreneurs must struggle with, understand and manage these problems now. We can't enjoy the leisurely dabbling permitted to market followers, but rather, we must perform the focused hard work required of career education leaders.

AICS must take the initiative and move quickly and decisively on the dropout and default issues. We must insist that unpleasant truths be faced by all participants in the debate lest "solutions" be imposed by reactionaries wearing the mask of reform. . . .

In short, the past may be prologue, but it must not be our blueprint for the future. In 1987 we AICS members must do what our predecessors did seventy-five years ago: join together and commit ourselves to a cooperative and creative effort to solve the problems that are tomorrow's opportunities. . . .

In the years ahead, we will be second to none in the educational programs in which we compete. We will be quality institutions our students can count on to provide exactly what they need, when and where they need it, at a competitive tuition cost. To achieve and maintain our competitive edge, we will serve our students with unsurpassed effectiveness and attention to detail. We will measure everything we do against the very best, and then reach for even higher quality and performance.

The past is indeed prologue. For AICS, the best is yet to come.

—Mary Ann Lawlor

Appendix C: AICS Officials

Chair of the Board

B. F. Williams	1912–1937
E. M. Hull	1938–1942
P. S. Spangler (NAACS)	1943
H. N. Rasely	
(War Emergency Council)	1943
H. N. Rasely (NCBS)	1944
Sanford L. Fisher	
(NAACS)	1945–1947
George A. Spaulding	
(NCBS)	1946–1947
George A. Meadows	
(NAACS)	1948–1950
E. R. Maetzold (NACBS)	1948–1950
Jay W. Miller	1950–1951
C. I. Blackwood	1951–1952
H. Everett Pope	1952–1953
J. K. Kincaid	1953–1954
Harold B. Post	1954–1955
I. W. Stevens	1955–1956
J. T. Vetter	1956–1957
H. O. Balls	1957–1958
Charles E. Palmer	1958–1959
Robert W. Sneden	1959–1960
Jack H. Jones	1961–1962
G. C. Stewart (UBSA)	1961–1962
Weldon L. Strawn (UBSA)	1961–1962
Hugh T. Barnes	1962–1963
Robert W. Sneden	1963–1964
Walter J. Tribbey	1964–1965
Clarence A. Phillips	1965–1966
C. D. Rohlffs	1966–1967
Harry G. Green	1967–1968
L. Clay Spencer	1968–1969
L. R. Stevens	1969–1970
Harry E. Ryan	1970–1971
Morris J. W. Gaebe	1971–1972
Carl W. Durham (AICS)	1972–1973
A. Lauren Rhude	1973–1974
Maurice F. Egan	1974–1975
Charles W. Davidson	1975–1976
Joe E. Lee	1976–1977
Larry L. Luing	1977–1978
John W. Hauer	1978–1979
Douglas Devaux	1979–1980
Jan V. Friedheim	1980–1981
John A. Yena	1981–1982
Frank Paone	1982–1983
Charles E. Palmer	1983–1984
A. R. Sullivan	1984–1985
Edward M. Shapiro	1985–1986
John T. South, Jr.	1986–1987
Mary Ann Lawlor	1987–1988

Chair of Accrediting Commission

John R. Humphreys	1953–1955
Jay W. Miller	1955–1957
C. H. Husson	1957–1959
Charles P. Harbottle	1959–1961
William J. Hamilton	1961–1962
Harold B. Post	1962–1964
Charles E. Palmer	1964–1965
Stuart E. Sears	1966
Harold B. Post	1967
Robert W. Sneden	1968
G. C. Stewart	1969
A. Lauren Rhude	1970
Douglas Devaux	1971
Jack H. Jones	1972
Larry L. Luing	1973
Ernest E. Roblee	1974
George J. Brennan, Jr.	1975
A. R. Sullivan	1976
Coleman T. Furr	1977
Jan V. Friedheim	1978
Prentiss Carnell III	1979
Edward M. Shapiro	1980
Dean Johnston	1981
Howard S. Steed	1982
Robert S. Kline	1983
C. Dexter Rohm	1984
F. Jack Henderson, Jr.	1985
John T. South, III	1986
Donald H. Waldbauer	1987

Appendix D: Members of the Century Club

In 1979, the AICS Board of Directors established the Century Club for AICS accredited institutions that have been serving students for 100 years or more. Certificates are issued annually to institutions qualifying for membership.

1840 Duff's Business Institute
      Pittsburgh, PA

1850 Detroit Business Institute
      Detroit, MI

1850 Ridley-Lowell School of Business
      Binghamton, NY

1854 Bryant & Stratton Business
      Institute, Inc.
      Buffalo, NY

1856 Madison Business College
      Madison, WI

1857 Albany Business College
      Albany, NY

1857 Indiana Business College
      Richmond, IN

1858 Davis Junior College of Business
      Toledo, OH

1859 Heffley & Browne Secretarial
      School
      Brooklyn, NY

1860 Morse School of Business
      Hartford, CT

1860 Miami-Jacobs Junior College of
      Business
      Dayton, OH

1862 Indiana Business College
      Terre Haute, IN

1862 Rockford Business College
      Rockford, IL

1863 Casco Bay College
      Portland, ME

1863 Milwaukee Stratton College
      Milwaukee, WI

1863 Rochester Business Institute
      Rochester, NY

1864 Stone School of Business
      New Haven, CT

1864 Sullivan Junior College of
      Business
      Louisville, KY

1865 Jacksonville Business and
      Careers Institute
      Jacksonville, IL

1866 United College
      Bridgeton, MO

1866 Mansfield Business College
      Mansfield, OH

1867 Jackson Business Institute
      Jackson, MI

1868 Sanford-Brown Business College
      St. Ann, MO

1869 Allentown Business School
      (National Education Center)
      Allentown, PA

1870 Gem City College
      Quincy, IL

1873 Drake Business School
      New York, NY

1873 Metropolitan School of Business
      Chicago, IL

1874 Minneapolis Business College
      Minneapolis, MN

1877 Minnesota School of Business
      Minneapolis, MN

1879 Burdett School
      Boston, MA

1879 Draughons Junior College of
      Business
      Nashville, TN

1879 Hickox School
      Boston, MA

1879 Platt College
      St. Joseph, MO

1879 Wood School
      New York, NY

1880 Northeastern School of
      Commerce
      Bay City, MI

1881 Hammel Actual College
      Akron, OH

1881 Excel College
      Clarksburg, WV

1882 Argubright Business College
      Battle Creek, MI

1882 Knoxville Business College
      Knoxville, TN

1882 Michiana College of Commerce
      South Bend, IN

1883 Cleary College
      Ypsilanti, MI

1883 Drake College of Business
      Elizabeth, NJ

1883 Indiana Business College
      Lafayette, IN

1883 Wichita Business College
      Wichita, KS

1884 Altoona School of Commerce
      Altoona, PA

1884 Erie Business Center
      Erie, PA

1884 Lincoln School of Commerce
      Lincoln, NE

1885 Du Bois Business College
      Du Bois, PA

1885 Globe College of Business
      St. Paul, MN

1885 McKenzie College
      Chattanooga, TN

1885 Palmer School
      Philadelphia, PA

1886 Jamestown Business College
      Jamestown, NY

1886 National Business College
      Salem, VA

Appendix E: AICS Awards

Distinguished Service Award

Presented annually to one or more individuals who have provided valuable service to the Association during that year.

1968   Charles W. Davidson

1969   Clarence A. Phillips
        Paul R. Jackson
        G. C. Stewart

1970   Sylvia Lepine
        Raymond W. Baxandall
        (posthumously)

1971   Charles W. Davidson
        A. Lauren Rhude
        Gerald C. Phillips
        Sue Berke King

1972   Alexander Sheff
        Burton Sheff

1973   Robert W. Sneden
        C. D. Rohlffs
        Donald S. Chaney

1974   Walter J. Tribbey

1975   Coleman Furr
        Richard H. Laube

1976   C. William Tayler

1977   John W. Hauer
        A. O. Sullivan

1978   Gertrude C. Shapiro
        F. Leland Watkins

1979   Arline H. Bunch
        Maurice F. Egan
        R. Louise Grooms
        Mary B. Wine

1980   Charles Gorman
        Jones Colleges
        H. Everett Pope, Sr.
        Sue Berke King
        Puerto Rico Assn of
            Independent Colleges and
            Schools

1981   Jan V. Eisenhour
        Larry L. Luing
        Urban Schools Committee
            Benedict O. Harris
            Ted Jakub
        Craig F. Johnson
        Richard S. Ross, Jr.
        James S. White

1982   Guy W. Tillet
        Jerry F. Daly (Special Merit)
        Richard J. Neat (Special Merit)

1983   Mary Ann Lawlor
        David S. Shefrin
        Eleanor P. Vreeland
        Madeleine B. Hemmings

1984   Robert S. Kline

1985   Maurice F. Egan
        Diane Scappaticci
        Warren T. Schimmel

1986   Victor K. Biebighauser
        John A. Yena

1987   Robert J. Nesbit

Distinguished Governmental Service Award

Given annually to an individual at either the state or national level who as a public employee has demonstrated a particular interest and understanding of the role of the independent school and college or the students who attend these institutions.

1973   Frank N. Albanese (Ohio)

1974   Joseph A. Clark (Indiana)

1975   Harold A. Shoberg (Arizona)

1976   Carol L. Wennerdahl (Illinois)

1977   David R. Jacobson
        (Connecticut)

1978   William E. O'Brien (Rhode
        Island)

1979   Alan R. Cullum (Tennessee)

1980   William F. Gaul, House
        Committee on Education &
        Labor (posthumously)

1981   James W. Moore, Student
        Financial Aid Assistance
        Program (U.S. Department of
        Education)

1982   Kenneth R. Reeher,
        Pennsylvania Higher
        Education Agency

1983   Edward M. Elmendorf,
        Assistant Secretary for
        Postsecondary Education
        (U.S. Department of
        Education)

        Robert C. Rogers (Maryland)

        Richard T. Jerue, National
        Commission on Student
        Financial Assistance

1984   Hon. Paul Simon, U.S. Senate
        (Illinois)

1985   Hon. Claiborne Pell, U.S.
        Senate (Rhode Island)

1986 Hon. Mario Biaggi, U.S. House
of Representatives
(New York, NY)

Laverne Borst (Pennsylvania)

Samuel Booker (Texas)

1987 Daniel R. Lau, Student
Financial Aid Programs
(U.S. Department of
Education)

Member-of-the-Year Award

Given annually to an individual whose
service during that year is of particular
significance to the organization, the
independent career education sector, or
to the students served by AICS member
institutions.

1968	Walter J. Tribbey
1969	Wayne W. Wiegert (posthumously)
1970	R. Louise Grooms
1971	LeRoy R. Stevens (posthumously)
1972	Keith Fenton
1973	Jack H. Jones
1974	Charles Gorman
1975	Donald S. Chaney
1976	Ernest E. Roblee
1977	Frank Paone
1978	Jan V. Eisenhour
1979	A. Lauren Rhude
1980	Howard S. Steed
1981	Morris J. W. Gaebe
1982	Charles W. Davidson
1983	Harry V. Weber
1984	Dexter Rohm
1985	A. R. Sullivan
1986	Charles E. Palmer
1987	Eleanor P. Vreeland

Distinguished Career Award

Given annually to one or more
individuals whose career, over a number
of years, has been distinguished by the
quality of the contribution to the field
of independent career education.

1983	John R. McCartan Robert W. Sneden
1984	Donald S. Chaney (posthumously) Charles P. Harbottle Jack H. Jones
1985	Harry E. Jerome (posthumously) Richard H. Laube (posthumously) Melvin T. Mergenhagen
1986	Leo Blackburn Ernest E. Roblee Jules Rosenblatt (posthumously)
1987	Maurice F. Egan

Special Recognition Award

1982	A. Dallas Martin, National Association of Student Financial Aid Administrators

Appendix F: References

Chapter 1

Accreditation Criteria, Accrediting Commission of the Association of Independent Colleges and Schools, Washington, DC, 1985.

AICS Handbook, Association for Independent Colleges and Schools, Washington, DC, January, 1987.

Association of Independent Colleges and Schools Annual Review and Forecast 1986 Edition, Association of Independent Colleges and Schools, Washington, DC, 1986.

Association of Independent Colleges and Schools (Brochure), Association of Independent Colleges and Schools, Washington, DC, 1984.

Directory of Educational Institutions, 1987, Association of Independent Colleges and Schools, Washington, DC, 1986.

Private Career Schools and Colleges, Association of Independent Colleges and Schools, Washington, DC, 1985.

Chapter 2

A Chronology of Business Education in the United States, National Business Education Association, Reston, VA, 1977.

Johnson, Charles A., "Proprietary Vocational Schools," *Developing the Nation's Work Force, Yearbook 5*, American Vocational Association, Washington, DC.

Miller, J. W., *A Critical Analysis of the Organization, Administration and Function of the Private Business Schools of the United States*, South-Western Publishing Company, Cincinnati, OH, 1939.

Miller, J. W., *The Independent Business School in American Education*, Gregg Division, McGraw-Hill Book Company, New York, NY, 1964.

Private Career Education—A National Resource in an Ever-Changing Society, Association of Independent Colleges and Schools, Washington, DC, 1985.

Reigner, Charles, G., *Beginnings of the Business School*, H.M. Rowe Company, Baltimore, MD, 1938.

Chapter 3

A Chronology of Business Education in the United States, National Business Education Association, Reston, VA, 1977.

Accredited News, National Association of Accredited Commercial Schools, Jamestown, New York, December 1911; May 1922; May 1923; August 1923; August 1924; June 1925;
December 1925; March 1926; May 1926; August 1926; May 1927; May 1928; October 1928; December 1928; September 1929; October 1929; July 1930; February 1931; July 1931; October 1931; December 1931; May 1932; February 1933; April 1933; September 1934; February 1935; July 1935; October 1935; November 1936; February 1937; November 1937; February 1938.

DECA: The First Thirty Years, American Vocational Association, Alexandria, VA, 1976.

Grun, Bernard, *The Timetables of History*, Simon & Schuster, New York, NY, 1964.

Sullivan, Mark, *Our Times*, Charles Scribners Sons, New York, NY, 1943.

Vocational Education Journal, American Vocational Association, Alexandria, VA, November, December, 1986.

Chapter 4

Accredited News, National Association of Accredited Commercial Schools, Jamestown, NY, February, 1937; February 1938; February 1939; February 1940; August 1940; May 1941; May 1942; August 1942; February 1943; August 1943; November 1945; June-August 1946; May 1947; May 1948; June 1949; August 1949; November 1949; January 1950.

Blackburn, Leo, Letter of April 17, 1987, Chillicothe, OH.

The Business School Executive, National Council of Business Schools, Washington, DC, 1945. September 1945; September 1946; March 1949; June 1949; March 1951; December 1952; June 1954; March 1959.

The Compass, American Association of Commercial Colleges, Burlington, IA, January, 1943; January 1959.

The Compass, United Business Schools Association, Washington, DC, May, 1952; August 1952; September 1952; October 1952; November 1952.

Directory of Business Schools, United Business Schools Association, Washington, DC, 1962-1963.

Chapter 5

AICS Handbook, Association of Independent Colleges and Schools, Washington, DC, 1987.

The Compass, published by United Business Schools Association and *AICS Compass*, published by The Association of Independent Colleges and Schools, Washington, DC, February, 1963; March 1963; July 1963; May 1964;
February 1965; March 1965; April 1965; April 1966; July 1966; April 1967; September 1967; November 1967; January 1968; May 1968; June 1968; December 1968; March 1969; April 1969; May 1969; June 1969; November 1969; February 1970; August 1970; October 1970; November 1971; February 1972; July 1972; February 1973; March 1973; September 1973; January 1974; May 1974; April 1975; May 1975; October 1975; April 1976; April 1977; June 1977; December 1977; September 1978; January 1979; May 1979; September 1979; October 1979; January 1980; February 1981; January 1982; March 1982; May 1982; July 1982; June 1983; September 1983; March 1984; May 1984; September 1984; November 1984; April 1985; October 1985; January 1986; October 1986; February 1987; April 1987.

Directory of Business Schools, United Business Schools Association, Washington, DC, 1962.

Chapter 6

Bell South Corporation 1986 Annual Report, Atlanta, GA, 1987.

"The Economy of the 1990's" Fortune, New York, NY, February 2, 1987.

Freidheim, Jan, "Where We're Going," Mobiltape Company, Inc., Glendale, CA, 1986.

Respondents to a survey prepared by Dr. George J. Petrello, February 1987: Marty Berry, Randy Berry, Leo Blackburn, Manuel H. Colomo, Dawn Conley, C. W. Davidson, James E. Deitz, Sharon Drain, Bernard H. Ehrlich, Steve Eisnaugle, Keith Fenton, Charles P. Harbottle, John Hauer, Jack H. Jones, Larry L. Luing, Sherry Perry, A. Lauren Rhude, John Riggs, Stuart E. Sears, Earle Sutton, John T. South, Weldon L. Strawn, Annita Thompson.

Toeffler, Alvin, ed., *Learning for Tomorrow: The Role of the Future in Education*, Vintage Books, New York, NY, 1974.

Yena, John A., "Where We're Going," Mobiltape Company, Inc., Glendale, CA, 1987.

Index

Shoberg, Harold A., 164
Shorthand, types of, 57–58
Simon, Paul (Senator), 164
Smith-Hughes Act, 73
Sneden, Robert W., 122, 160, 162, 164, 165
South, John T., Jr., 160, 162
South, John T., III, 36, 162
South College, *11*
Southeastern Business College, 102
Southeastern Business College Association, 107
Southern Accredited Business Colleges, 97
Southern Business Education Association, 88
South-Western Publishing Co., 38, 73, 107, 135
Spangler, P. S., Dr., 65, 100, 162
Spaulding, George A., 98, 162
Special Recognition Award, winner of, 165
Spencer, Enos, 65
Spencer, L. Clay, 162
Spencer, Platt Rogers, 57, 59
Spencerian Commercial Academy, 57
Spencerian Commercial School, 65
Spencerian Shorthand, 57
Sports, at AICS member schools, 131
Steed, C. C., 128
Steed, Howard S., 162, 165
Stenographic machines, 135

Stenotype machine, 58
Stevens, I. W., 162
Stevens, LeRoy R., 162, 165
Stevens-Henager College of Business, *13*
Stewart, G. C., 107, 125, 127, 134, 162, 164
Stone School of Business, 163
Student Financial Aid Administration Committee, 43
Students, assessment of by AICS, 39–40
Stratton, H. B., 59, 60
Strawn, Weldon L., 107, 160, 162
Strayer College, 98
Sullivan, A. O., 164
Sullivan, A. R., 125, 160, 162, 165
Sullivan Business College, 131
Sullivan Junior College, 131
Sullivan Junior College of Business, *15*, 125, 163
Sweetland, Dean C., 107

Tampa Business College, 89, 98
Tayler, C. William, 164
Taylor, James R., Dr., 127
Teachers, training of by AICS, 38–39
Temple schools, 133–134
Theta Alpha Chi, 96
Tillet, Guy W., 164
Toren, Robert M., 128
Tribbey, Walter J., 107, 160, 162, 164, 165
Trenary, Otis L., 65

Treu, Gretchen, *8*
Typewriters
  invention of, 58
  wartime demand for, 99–100

United Business Education Association (UBEA), 88, 89
United Business Schools Association (UBSA)
  becomes AICS, 120
  enrollments of schools in, 120
  founding of, 107–108
  government relations of, 121–122
  and other organizations, 135
  see also American Association of Commercial Colleges; Association of Independent Colleges and Schools; National Association of Accredited Commercial Schools
United College, 163
United States Bureau of Education, 74, 79, 80
United States Civil Service Commission, 80, 100, 108, 109
United States Office of Education, 100
Utica School of Commerce, *57, 76, 85*

Van Opt, B. H., 82
Veterans, education of, 80, 101–103, 123
Veterans Affairs and Military Education Committee, 43

Vetter, J. T., 162
Vigilance Committee, 74, 81
Vocational Education Act, 120
Voyles, Bonnie, 36
Vreeland, Eleanor P., 36, 164, 165

Waldbauer, Donald H., 162
Walker, Charles, 96
War Emergency Council, of NAACS and AACC, 98–100, 104
Waterloo Business College, 65
Watkins, F. Leland, 164
Watson, W. N., 65, 74
Waukegan Business College, 65
Weber, Harry V., 165
Wennerdahl, Carol L., 164
White, James C., 164
White House Conference on Education (1952), 103–104
Wichita Business College, 163
Wiegert, Wayne W., 165
Wilkes-Barre Business College, 65
Williams, Benjamin Franklin, 63, 64, 74, 78, 83–84, 98, 104, 106, 107, 162
Williams, Pat (Representative), 36
Wine, Mary B., *7, 9, 40*, 129, 160, 164
Women, in business, 58, 85
Woods, Jacqueline, *7*
Wood School, 163
Woodward, C. W., 97, 98, 99, 136

Yena, John A., *144, 152*, 162, 164

Picture Credits

The publisher gratefully acknowledges the many individuals and institutions who contributed illustrations for inclusion in this book.

Frontmatter
ii: John Fogle/The Picture Cube; vi: © 1987 Tom Dunham; 1: Matthew Klein; 2: © 1987 Tom Dunham; 3: © 1987 Tom Dunham.

Photo Essay: AICS at Work
All photos © 1987 Tom Dunham except page 8 (bottom left): Davis Photographic Associates, Inc.

Photo Essay: AICS—Service Through Diversity
10 (top left): Schiller International University; 10 (top right, bottom): AICS; 11 (top): Brooks Institute; 11 (center): Cannon's International Business College of Honolulu; 11 (bottom left): Huertas Junior College; 11 (bottom right): South College; 12 (top): Johnson & Wales College; 12 (center, bottom): AICS; 13 (top, center left): AICS; 13 (center right): Schiller International University; 13 (bottom): Barnes Business College; 14 (top): Schiller International University; 14 (center left): International Business College; 14 (center right): San Diego Golf Academy; 14 (bottom): Jamestown Business College; 15 (top): Schiller International University; 15 (center left): Sullivan Junior College of Business; 15 (center right): Hagerstown Business College; 15 (bottom): AICS.

Photo Essay: AICS—Students in Action
16 (top left): Richard Hackett/Direct Positive Images; 16 (top center): Charles Fell/FPG; 16 (top right): Direct Positive Images; 16 (bottom): Lawrence Migdale/Photo Researchers, Inc.; 17 (top): Stacy Pick/Stock-Boston; 17 (center left): Jeffery Sylvester/FPG; 17 (center right): Will Faller/Direct Positive Images; 17 (bottom): Cannon's International College of Honolulu; 18 (top left): Bob Daemmrich/Stock-Boston; 18 (top right): Bill Gallery/Stock-Boston; 18 (bottom): Dan Walsh/The Picture Cube; 19 (top): John Terence/FPG; 19 (center) Jon Goell/The Picture Cube; 19 (bottom): Jo Sloan/The Picture Cube; 20 (top): Fashion Institute of Design and Merchandising; 20 (center): Will Faller/Direct Positive Images; 20 (bottom left): ©1987 Tom Dunham; 20 (bottom right): Joseph Nettis/Photo Researchers, Inc.; 21 (top): Cannon's International Business College of Honolulu; 21 (center): Richard Rutchings/Photo Researchers, Inc.; 21 (bottom): Academy of Floral Design; 22 (top): Hagerstown Business College; 22 (center): Roger Miller/The Image Bank; 22 (bottom): Spencer Grant/The Picture Cube; 23 (top): D. C. Lowe/FPG; 23 (center): Windsor Puzl/Alpha; 23 (bottom): Ann McQueen/The Picture Cube; 24 (top): Joyce Photographics/Photo Researchers, Inc.; 24 (center): John Colletti/The Picture Cube; 24 (bottom): Bill Gallery/Stock-Boston; 25 (top): Frank Siteman/The Picture Cube; 25 (center): Jeffrey W. Myers/FPG; 25 (bottom left): Visual Education; 25 (bottom right): Jim Pickerell/FPG.

Introduction: Let's Celebrate
28 (top): Davis Photographic Associates, Inc.; 28 (bottom): AICS; 29 (top): Chaparral Career College; 29 (bottom left): AICS; 29 (bottom right): Johnson & Wales College.

Chapter I: The Mission
30: AICS; 32 (top): Bob Owen/AICS; 32 (bottom): ©1987 Tom Dunham; 33 (top): Madison Business College; 33 (center): Johnson & Wales College; 33 (bottom): Triton College/AICS; 34 (top): Madison Business College; 34 (bottom): ©1987 Tom Dunham; 35: ©1987 Tom Dunham; 36 (both): AICS; 37 (top): Bob Rogers/Direct Positive Images; 37 (bottom): ©1987 Tom Dunham; 38 (bottom): AICS; 39 (top): AICS; 39 (bottom): Madison Business College; 40 (both): ©1987 Tom Dunham; 41: AICS; 42 (top): AICS; 42 (bottom): ©1987 Tom Dunham; 43: AICS;

44 (top): Ted Buel/Fashion Institute of Design and Merchandising; 44 (center, bottom): Central Pennsylvania Business School; 45 (top, bottom right): Central Pennsylvania Business School; 45 (bottom left): Fashion Institute of Design and Merchandising.

Chapter 2: Genesis and Roots
46: AICS; 48: Albany Business College; 49: Albany Business College; 50 (all): Library of Congress; 51 (top): From the collections of Henry Ford Museum and Greenfield Village; 51 (center): Ford Motor Company; 51 (bottom): NASA; 52 (top): Library of Congress; 52 (bottom): Bettmann Archive; 53 (top): Culver Pictures; 53 (center): Bettmann Archive; 53 (bottom): courtesy of the New York Historial Society; 54 (top): Museum of Modern Art, Film Stills Archive; 54 (bottom left): Culver Pictures; 54 (bottom right): Library of Congress; 55 (top left, bottom): Library of Congress; 55 (top right): courtesy of the New York Historical Society; 56: Duff's Business Institute; 57 (top): Johnson & Wales College; 57 (bottom): Utica School of Commerce; 58: Gregg Division/McGraw-Hill Book Company; 59 (both): Miami-Jacobs Junior College; 60: Central Pennsylvania Business School; 61 (both): Central Pennsylvania Business School.

Chapter 3: Reaching for Silver (1912—1937)
62: Ohio Valley Business College; 64 (top): *Accredited News* (February 1938); 64 (bottom): Jamestown Business College; 65: Miami-Jacobs Junior College; 66 (top, bottom left): Library of Congress; 66 (bottom right): Bettmann Archive; 67 (top): State Archives of Michigan; 67 (bottom): Bettmann Archive; 68 (top): Copyright ©1912 by The *New York Times Company*. Reprinted by permission. 68 (bottom): AP-Wide World Photos; 69 (top): AP-Wide World Photos; 69 (bottom): Library of Congress; 70 (top): Bettmann Archive; 70 (bottom left): UPI-Bettmann Newsphotos; 70 (bottom right): Library of Congress; 71 (top): The Museum of Modern Art/Walt Disney Productions; 71 (center): The Museum of Modern Art/Film Stills Archive; 71 (bottom): Archives of Labor & Urban Affairs/Wayne State University; 72: Library of Congress; 73: Miami-Jacobs Junior College; 74: International Business College; 75: *Accredited News* (December 1929); 76 (top): Utica School of Commerce; 76 (bottom): *Accredited News* (February 1936); 77 (top): *Accredited News* (February 1921); 77 (bottom): Central Pennsylvania Business School; 78: Utica School of Commerce; 79: Duff's Business Institute; 81 (top): Parks College; 81 (bottom): Draughon's Business College; 82: Miami-Jacobs Junior College; 83: *Accredited News*; 84: *Accredited News* (February 1921); 85: Utica School of Commerce.

Chapter 4: On to the Gold (1937–1962)
86: Brook's Institute; 88: Robinson Business College; 89 (top): Ohio Valley Business College; 89 (bottom): Tampa Business College; 90 (both): Library of Congress; 91 (top): Museum of Modern Art/Film Stills Archive; 91 (bottom left): Library of Congress; 91 (bottom right): Museum of Modern Art/Film Stills Archive; 92 (top): AP-Wide World Photos; 92 (center): John Phillips, *Life Magazine* © Time, Inc.; 92 (bottom): by permission of Bill Mauldin and Wil-Jo Associates, Inc.; 93 (top): Alfred Eisenstaedt, *Life Magazine* © Time, Inc.; 93 (center): National Archives; 93 (bottom): UPI-Bettmann Newsphotos; 94 (top, bottom): AP-Wide World Photos; 94 (center): UPI-Bettmann Newsphotos; 95 (top): Whammo, Inc.; 95 (center): Los Angeles Dodgers; 95 (bottom): AP-Wide World Photos; 96: National Business College; 97: AP-Wide World Photos; 98: Tampa Business College; 99 (top): *The Compass* (January 1945); 99 (bottom): Ohio Valley Business College; 100: Central Pennsylvania Business School; 102: Draughon's Business College; 103 (top): Draughon's Business College; 103 (bottom): International Business College; 104: Miami-Jacobs Junior College, 105: Miami-Jacobs Junior College;

106: Huertas Junior College; 108: *The Compass* (May 1962); 109: Draughon's Business College.

Chapter 5: Prospecting for a Diamond (1962–1987)
110: Johnson & Wales College; 112: Robinsons Business College; 113 (top): Parks College; 113 (bottom): *The Compass* (December 1979); 114 (top left): Library of Congress; 114 (top right): AP-Wide Word Photos; 114 (bottom): NASA; 115 (top, bottom): AP-Wide World Photos; 115 (center): National Archives; 116 (top): Paul Conklin; 116 (center): Nixon Project/National Archives; 116 (bottom): UPI-Bettmann Newsphotos; 117 (top): National Archives; 117 (center): UPI-Bettmann Newsphotos; 117 (bottom): AP-Wide World Photos; 118 (top): AP-Wide World Photos; 118 (bottom): Bill Clark/National Park Service; 118–119 (top): AP-Wide World Photos; 118–119 (bottom): UPI-Bettmann Newsphotos; 119 (top): © 1977 Lucasfilm Ltd. All Right Reserved; 119 (bottom): AP-Wide World Photos; 120: Johnson & Wales College; 121: Johnson & Wales College; 122: Johnson & Wales College; 123: Parks School of Business; 124: International Business College; 125 (both): New Hampshire College; 126: Johnson & Wales College; 127: Sanford-Brown College; 128: AICS; 129: Brooks Institute; 130: *The Compass* (April 1979); 131: Madison Business College; 133 (both): College of Legal Arts; 134: *AICS Compass* (April 1985); 135 (top): Sanford-Brown College; 135 (bottom): *The Compass* (March 1979); 136: Rider College; 137 (both): Brooks Institute.

Chapter 6: The Future
138: Johnson & Wales College; 140 (top): Donald Dietz; 140 (bottom): David A. Krathwohl; 141 (top): Robert Morris College; 141 (bottom): © 1987 Harlee Little; 142 (top): Peter Menzel; 142 (bottom): James Franklin; 143: Cannon's International Business College of Honolulu; 144 (top): Cannon's International Business College of Honolulu; 144 (bottom): Miami-Jacobs Junior College; 145: Atlantic Community College; 146 (both): Caguas City College; 147: Brian Lewis; 148 (top): Miami-Jacobs Junior College; 148 (bottom): © 1987 Harlee Little; 149: Central Pennsylvania Business School; 150: Atlantic Community College; 151 (top): Central Pennsylvania Business School; 151 (bottom): Madison Business College; 152: AICS; 153 (top): adapted from *AICS Compass*; 154: AICS; 155: Atlantic Community College; 156: Central Pennsylvania Business School; 157 (top): Miami-Jacobs Junior College; 157 (bottom): Randy Matusow; 159 (top): AICS; 159 (center): The Berkeley Schools; 159 (bottom): Madison Business College.

Endmatter
161: © 1987 Tom Dunham.